SURVIVING LAMENTATIONS

SURVIVING LAMENTATIONS

CATASTROPHE, LAMENT, AND PROTEST IN THE AFTERLIFE OF A BIBLICAL BOOK

Tod Linafelt

THE UNIVERSITY OF CHICAGO PRESS
CHICAGO & LONDON

Tod Linafelt is assistant professor of biblical studies at Georgetown University, author of a commentary on Ruth for the series *Berit Olam* (1999), and coeditor of *God in the Fray: A Tribute to Walter Brueggemann* (1998, with Timothy K. Beal).

The University of Chicago Press, Chicago 60637
The University of Chicago Press, Ltd., London

© 2000 by The University of Chicago
All rights reserved. Published 2000

Printed in the United States of America
09 08 07 06 05 04 03 02 01 00   1 2 3 4 5

ISBN: 0-226-48190-5 (cloth)

Portions of chapter 7 originally appeared in "The Impossibility of Mourning," in *God in the Fray: A Tribute to Walter Brueggemann*, ed. Tod Linafelt and Timothy K. Beal (Minneapolis: Augsburg Fortress, 1998). Copyright © 1998 Augsburg Fortress; reprinted by permission.

Library of Congress Cataloging-in-Publication Data

Linafelt, Tod, 1965–
    Surviving Lamentations : catastrophe, lament, and protest in the afterlife of a biblical book / Tod Linafelt.
        p.   cm.
    Includes bibliographical references and index.
    ISBN 0-226-48190-5 (cloth : alk. paper)
    1. Bible. O.T. Lamentations—Criticism, interpretation, etc. 2. Bible. O.T. Lamentations—Criticism, interpretation, etc., Jewish. 3. Survival in literature. I. Title.

BS1535.2.L56 2000
224'.306—dc21   99-056022

♾ The paper used in this publication meets the minimum requirements of the American National Standard for Information Sciences—Permanence of Paper for Printed Library Materials, ANSI Z39.48-1992.

to my mother,
Elizabeth Madden

Contents

Acknowledgments

Much of the initial research for this book was undertaken during a year (1994–95) spent at the Oxford Centre for Hebrew and Jewish Studies. My work there benefitted greatly from conversations with Glenda Abramson, Philip Alexander, Tim S. F. Horner, Jennifer Koosed, Yvonne Sherwood, and Dalia Yasharpour. I was very lucky as well to have Jeremy Schonfield read an early draft of my work and give me extensive feedback.

A more complete version was read by David Blumenthal, Walter Brueggemann, and John Hayes, all of whom provided extensive and helpful comments on how it might be improved. I am also grateful to a number of people who, over the last few years, have graciously read and responded to parts of the manuscript or rough drafts of various chapters, including Tim Beal, David Gunn, Gary Phillips, Chip Dobbs-Allsopp, Kathleen O'Connor, David Stern, Nancy Lee, Pam Reich, Brentonio Plate, Chris Boesel, the late Jean-François Lyotard, and the Tel Mac group.

The person to whom I am most indebted is undoubtedly Carol Newsom, who repeatedly pushed me to clarify my thinking and sharpen my arguments; she remains for me a model of how a scholar can be both rigorous and open to interpretive risk. I am thankful, as always, for the presence of Rebecca Nelson Linafelt, and now for our daughter Eleanor; they will no doubt be glad to see this book finally make it into print! For which fact I am obliged to Alan Thomas, executive editor at the University of Chicago Press, for encouragement and for his careful editorial work, as well as to assistant editor Randolph Petilos.

Finally, there remains only to express my gratitude to my mother, Elizabeth Madden, who continues to read everything that I write and whose opinion I will always value. I am pleased to be able to dedicate this book to her, though I will not pretend that it even begins to repay the debt that I owe her.

How to Survive the Book of Lamentations

The need to let suffering speak is the condition of all truth.

Theodor Adorno

One wonders how many ever read this book! In the old days when the Bible was read through from cover to cover at daily devotions, Lamentations was undoubtedly read. But how many really enjoyed it? Why should such a book be in the Bible?

W. P. Merrill

In the wake of the Holocaust and at the close of a century that has witnessed mass destruction and killings on an unprecedented scale, "survival" has become a pervasive and defining term of our era. The word has come to be used not only in reference those individuals and communities that have survived attempts at annihilation and genocide but also as a metaphor that has insinuated itself into literary theory and philosophy. This book draws on both of these senses of survival, the literal and the metaphorical, as a way of reinterpreting the biblical book of Lamentations and reconstruing its central role in the history of Jewish literary response to catastrophe. In conversation with a growing body of writings known as "literature of survival" (especially the work of Jean Améry, Bruno Bettelheim, Terrence Des Pres, and Robert J. Lifton) and with literary and philosophical reflections on "the survival of literature" (especially as articulated by Walter Benjamin, Jacques Derrida, and Jean-François Lyotard), I present Lamentations both as an ancient example of the

1

literature of survival and as a strikingly appropriate test case for contemporary theoretical discussions of how works of art and literature
can overrun their borders and generate their own "afterlife" in other
works that survive them.

   "One wonders how many ever read this book," writes the biblical commentator W. P. Merrill in the epigraph above. Surviving
Lamentations is, admittedly, no easy task. A more relentlessly brutal
piece of writing is scarcely imaginable. This short biblical book affronts the reader with a barrage of harsh and violent images: from its
opening portrayal of the city of Jerusalem as an abandoned widow
exposed to endless dangers, to the broken man of chapter three, to
the bleak description in chapter four of the inhabitants of a devas-
tated city, to the final unanswered appeal of chapter five, the reader
is not so much engaged by the book of Lamentations as assaulted by
it. Given its unsparing focus on destruction, pain, and suffering, one
might expect that Theodor Adorno's dictum, cited as the other epigraph to this chapter, would be easily met by those who have written on Lamentations. It is logical to expect that interpretations of the
book of Lamentations, more than those of any other biblical book,
would value the expression of pain, if not as "a condition of truth"
then at least as a mode of discourse with merit in and of itself. While
this has been the case in the history of interpretation of the book
(and more specifically the history of Jewish interpretation), critical
readings in the modern era have almost unanimously attempted to
tone down, expunge, or belittle the language of lament and anguish.

   The devaluing of the lament is, in my judgment, a strategy for
"surviving" Lamentations—that is, for the reader to somehow deal
with the pain and devastation represented by the book, especially as
it challenges the reader's theology or notions of how religious language should properly sound. This reading strategy most often is
manifested in the passing over or dismissal of the most disturbing or
accusatory passages in favor of the few passages that seem to evidence
hope through penitence and a reconciliation with God. So the majority of modern interpreters are eager to move quickly through
chapters 1 and 2 in order to light upon chapter 3. In chapters 1 and
2 of the book of Lamentations, Zion is personified as a widow and a
mother lamenting her suffering and perishing children. Her rhetoric is acutely urgent, in particular as it addresses God, from whom

Zion demands a response on behalf of her children. In contrast to
Zion, the suffering man of chapter 3 presents a decidedly less tena-
cious figure, one that seems to exhibit a more submissive posture toward suffering and a reticence to demand anything from God. And
unlike the Zion figure, who never receives the answer she demands
and thus never moves beyond lament, the suffering man of chapter
3 provides at least a semblance of hope:

> I call this to mind,
>> and I have hope:
> the Lord's faithfulness has not ended,
>> his compassion is not spent. (3:21–22)[1]

That this brief statement of "hope" is little more than the ghost of
salvation oracles past is scarcely mentioned by the commentators for
whom chapter 3 occupies a central and defining position for the
book as a whole. Modern scholars have tended latch onto this section of chapter 3, with its suffering yet (relatively) hopeful man,
which they then proclaim as the "high point"[2] or the "ideological
core"[3] of the book. By so doing, they evade the question of how the
figure of Zion might challenge and/or enrich modern interpretive
and theological discourse.[4]

   A second strategy taken by readers in order to "survive" Lamentations, in contrast to the evasion or devaluing of lament language,
is to face squarely the most disturbing and accusatory passages and
to attempt a direct answer to them. This is the strategy that one sees
repeatedly in the history of Jewish interpretation of the book, a history that has paid scant attention to the suffering man of chapter 3
but has expended great interpretive energy in trying to respond to
the demanding rhetoric of Zion from chapters 1 and 2. It is this second strategy with which the present study is principally concerned.
In the history of interpretation of Lamentations, the failure of God
to address Zion's petitions has generated an exegetical trajectory in
which text after text has identified Zion's concern for her children as
of primary significance and has attempted to provide the missing response. In this study I will trace the drive to supplement and thus to
"keep alive" the book of Lamentations as it is manifested in the subsequent Jewish texts of Second Isaiah, the targum to Lamentations
(an ancient translation from Hebrew into Aramaic), the midrash to

Lamentations (a collection of rabbinic commentary on the book), the medieval Hebrew poetry of Eleazar ben Kallir, and a contemporary short story by Cynthia Ozick.

My focus on the Zion figure from chapters 1 and 2 of Lamentations arises, first of all, from a close reading of the biblical text, as I will show in chapter two of this study. Emerging from this reading is an ancient text that, contrary to the consensus of biblical scholars, is more about the *expression* of suffering than the meaning behind it, more about the vicissitudes of *survival* than the abstractions of sin and guilt, and more about *protest* as a religious posture than capitulation or confession. My sense that Zion is a much more compelling figure than modern scholars have acknowledged finds support in those texts from the history of interpretation, mentioned above and explicated in the chapters that will follow, that have also deemed the figure of Zion to be worthy of literary and theological attention.

Having arrived at my focus on Zion and her children through a close reading of the text, however, I must admit that another motivation for a sustained literary and theological analysis of this trope comes into play. That is, I hope to counteract the pervasive devaluing of chapters 1 and 2 in favor of chapter 3, which has led, in my judgment, to a similar devaluing of the book of Lamentations as a resource for contemporary theological and literary works that must grapple with the implications of the Holocaust and other twentieth-century acts of mass atrocity. Claims that suffering is a punishment for sin or that a submissive spirit is more important than the voicing of pain and grief have become, at the end of the twentieth century (a century that Elizabeth Bishop has famously called "our worst yet") increasingly untenable, if not patently indefensible. So it is no surprise that a biblical book that is seen to advocate such a stance is largely ignored by writers attempting to respond with integrity to the complex problems posed to philosophical, literary, and theological practice by such acts of atrocity. It is my conviction that we are the poorer for this; for the figure of Zion, as I intend this study to demonstrate, offers a powerful alternative model of biblical theology to the "patient sufferer" of Lamentations 3. In the end this ancient text seems uncannily relevant to contemporary discourse on survival.

The Figure of the "Suffering Man" as a Model for Theological Interpretation

The focus in nineteenth- and twentieth-century Lamentations scholarship on the suffering man of chapter 3 is variously motivated.
There are at least three perceivable biases at play in such a focus: (1) a
male bias toward the male figure of chapter 3; (2) a Christian bias
toward the suffering man of Lamentations based on a perceived similarity to the figure of Christ; and (3) a broader emphasis on reconciliation with God rather than confrontation.

Chapter 3 of Lamentations begins with the statement "I am the
man" (אני הגבר). It is a phrase that could just as easily begin virtually every modern commentary on the book of Lamentations. Until the last decade or so, one could search in vain for citations in
the scholarly literature of commentaries on the book written by
women.[5] It is difficult to assess precisely how much the gender of an
interpreter affects the nature of the interpretation, yet it seems clear
that the maleness of the figure in chapter 3 has exerted an influence
on the evaluations of male interpreters. Consider Delbert Hillers's re-
marks, in the second edition (1992) of his well-known Anchor Bible
commentary, on how the suffering man figure of chapter 3 is presented as a model to be imitated:

> The book offers, in its central chapter, the example of an unnamed man
> who has suffered under the hand of God. To sketch this typical sufferer,
> this "Everyman," it draws on the language and ideas of the psalms of in-
> dividual lament, a tradition quite separate from the national history.
> From near despair this man wins through to confidence that God's mercy
> is not at an end, and that his final, inmost will for man is not suffering.
> From this beginning in hope the individual turns to call the nation to
> penitent waiting for God's mercy.[6]

Were this the 1972 edition of Hillers's commentary one might more
easily dismiss the gender-specific language as time-bound. Indeed, I
think that it is clear by his reference to God's "inmost will for *man*"
that he has "humanity" in mind as those to whom the strongman is
held out as a model. However, it is also clear that in choosing the
concept of an "Everyman" to express what he considers to be the

central message of the book, Hillers has effectively ruled out the possibility of using the figure of Zion to express such a message. One
could debate whether his concept of an Everyman led him to see
chapter 3 as the "high point" of the book or that his valuing of chapter 3 came first and found expression in the concept of an Everyman.
In either case, the results are the same: while an Everyman figure can
be taken as a model for all "humanity," the female figure of Zion cannot be construed as an Everyman.

This bias toward the strongman on the basis of gender is also
apparent in Alan Mintz's treatment of Lamentations. Mintz offers an
uncommonly compelling reading of chapters 1 and 2, one that
attends to the figure of Zion and acknowledges her language of
lament to a degree seldom seen. His reading has been quite influential for my own focus on Zion. Yet even so sensitive an interpreter as
Mintz falls into a stereotypical comparison and evaluation of Zion
and the suffering man based on gender.

> First there is a female figure, Fair Zion, used to emblemize the experience
> of victimization, and then a male figure, who is used to represent the
> struggle for theological reconciliation.[7]

The female figure is assigned the role of "victim," while the male figure is assigned the role of "theologian," thus eliding the fact that the
man is also presented as victimized and that Zion may be construed
as doing theology. Moreover, this characterization of the two figures
cannot be seen simply as a sort of division of labor, wherein each is
given a different but equally important role to play, for Mintz makes
a point of identifying chapter 3 as the "monumental center" and the
"theological nub" of the book of Lamentations.

Mintz attributes the preference for the male figure to the biblical
text itself, which he sees as making a conscious move from "the pain
that derives from the immediate experience of starvation, humilia-
tion and loss of life" to the "deeper and more abiding pain" of the
breakdown of meaning: "To deal with the loss of meaning . . . Zion
as a figure is simply not sufficient; a woman's voice, according to the
cultural code of Lamentations, can achieve expressivity but not reflection."[8] For Mintz, this move from the bodily and emotional to the
mental and intellectual necessitates the invention of "a new male figure . . . whose preference for theologizing rather than weeping is

demonstrated throughout."[9] In another context, I would wish to question the presupposition that the pain associated with the loss of meaning is deeper and more abiding than the pain experienced in starvation or the loss of life (which should be more appropriately identified in the context of the book of Lamentations as *violent* death), but for the purposes of this study it is enough to point out how such a presupposition is used to justify a preference for chapter 3 over chapters 1 and 2, which may in fact be attributable more to the interpreter than to the text. For example, though Mintz bases his judgment that chapter 3 is the theological nub of the book of Lamentations on the perceived move away from Zion's emotionalism and toward the "reasoning and cognition" of the man, he notes later that in 3:48–50 the male figure "goes on to declare his intention to weep incessantly until God takes pity on His people" and that the culmination of the chapter takes place when the suffering man achieves a "capacity for empathy" and becomes an "advocate of his people's cause before God."[10] In other words, the male figure abandons a theologizing based on reason and cognition for a theological stance not unlike that of Zion in chapters 1 and 2. The possibility that Zion voices the more powerful appeal is not considered by Mintz, though this possibility is supported by the history of interpretation, in which chapters 1 and 2 have received the most sustained attention and have generated the textual supplements that attempt to provide God's response.

The field of modern critical scholarship has been dominated not only by men, but more specifically by Christian men. This adds another bias in favor of Lamentations 3. Modern interpreters have not so much claimed that Lamentations actually refers knowingly to Jesus—as for example Justin Martyr did with Lamentations 4:20, which he read from the Septuagint (the Greek translation of the Hebrew Scriptures) in his first apology as "The breath of our life is Jesus Christ"[11]—rather they have associated the *type* of suffering and the submissive response that they find in chapter 3 with what is perceived as a similar type of suffering and response in the Passion narratives of the Gospels.

An example of this sort of linkage between the suffering of the man of Lamentations and that of Christ can be seen in the reflections of Walter Adenay:

As the supreme sufferer, he is also the representative sufferer . . . He has
gathered into himself the vast and terrible woes of his people. Thus he
foreshadows our Lord in his passion. We cannot but be struck with the
aptness of much in this third elegy when it is read in the light of the last
scenes of the gospel.[12]

Adenay may well be correct in his evaluation of this chapter's "aptness" in relation to the Passion narratives; yet it is no doubt just this
aptness that has contributed to the frequent decision that chapter 3
should consequently be given more interpretive weight than the
other chapters in the book. Consider also the comments of W. P. Merrill concerning the question of suffering addressed in Lamentations:

Christian men and women, of course, have an answer which far surpasses
any other, in that their leader, their Lord, their object of faith, is one who
suffered so terribly that he cried out, "My God, My God . . . ?"[13]

It is little wonder that Merrill, like so many other interpreters, opines
that only in chapter 3 do "we sound the depth and approach the climax of this little book."[14] A more recent commentary by S. Paul
Re'emi continues to make explicit reference to Christ as a key for in-
terpreting Lamentations. Referring to the events through which he
imagines the poet of Lamentations must have lived, Re'emi writes that
they "stand as historical fact for later generations to seek to understand
in the light of God's later intervention in the history of his people in
the Cross of Christ."[15] Re'emi's use of the cross of Christ here is almost
a textbook definition of what biblical scholars call a hermeneutical key
(i.e., a perspective that tightly governs how one reads a text).

The treatments of Lamentations by Adenay, Merrill, and Re'emi
were written, it should be pointed out, for an explicitly Christian audience, as volumes in The Expositor's Bible, The Interpreter's Bible, and
the International Theological Commentary, respectively. Thus perhaps one
should not make too much of the connections they suggest to Jesus
Christ. But the fact that this Christian bias seeps subtly into what is
normally thought of as more objective, critical scholarship can be
seen in the important commentary of Hans-Joachim Kraus. Like so
many others, Kraus deems chapter 3 to be "the true high point of
Lamentations." In particular, Kraus is drawn toward the two "individual laments" in 3:1–33 and 52–66, which are not merely personal but archetypal in nature. Chapter 3 serves as a "model" of suf-

fering that goes beyond its original utterance to include the suffering of the larger community, represented for example in the first-person plural voice of 3:40–47. Kraus explicitly relates the weaving together of collective and individual complaint in Lamentations 3 to the way in which the Christian community's triumph over sorrow is inspired by and joined with the triumph achieved by Jesus' Passion and death. The "good news" that the Christian reader can expect to find in Lamentations comes on the heels of the "rejection of grumbling"[16] in favor of accepting the "message of salvation" found in the overcoming of suffering. If even so well respected a critical scholar as Kraus can import this much Christian language and imagery into his treatment of Lamentations, one can safely surmise that a Christian bias in favor of chapter 3 based on Christological considerations is operative elsewhere as well, even when not so explicit as the above examples. As stated earlier, this bias in modern times is less likely to take the form of a simple identification of the suffering man with Christ, as it may have in precritical exegesis. Nevertheless, to the extent that the theological imagination of Christian biblical interpreters has been shaped by the notion of a suffering individual, who serves in some way as a model of redemption for others, their attention is understandably drawn to what is perceived as a similar figure in the masculine figure rather than the figure of Zion.

While it is clear in my judgment that both male and Christian biases have played a part in the ubiquitous preference for chapter 3 in modern readings of Lamentations, there is another bias that is shared by nearly all modern biblical interpreters, both male and female, Jewish and Christian. This third and more pervasive factor is the preference for submission and reconciliation vis-à-vis God. This preference is most characteristically expressed by a dual focus on the theological categories of guilt and hope. Robert Gordis writes:

> The poet shares a conviction in the righteousness and power of God, a trust in the saving virtue of repentance, and a faith that God's love will bring forgiveness and restoration.[17]

This statement serves as a good representative example of the dual focus on guilt and hope, inasmuch as it makes clear the connection between the two: there can be no hope without a recognition of guilt. So Renate Brandscheidt states in no uncertain terms: "Before there can be a favorable response to the lament, one thing must be clear to the people: that Yʜᴡʜ has ordained the punishment on account of the sins of the people."[18]

The concept of guilt functions for interpreters as a way of retaining the notion of God as the author of the destruction—something that can scarcely be avoided when reading Lamentations 1:12–15 and 2:1–9—while nevertheless relieving God of any ultimate responsibility for the disturbing results of the destruction: "He is declared righteous in His judgment."[19] Indeed, with the focus on guilt the destruction itself falls away nearly altogether. "The lament does not concern pain as such; rather, pain is the backdrop for the recognition of guilt, which is the real issue of a lament."[20] In such a strategy for reading there is no place for either the extensive descriptions of pain and destruction or the accusations of Zion toward God, both of which the reader encounters in chapters 1 and 2. The effect of this strategy can be seen in a recent study by Paul Ferris. Though admitting that the two main motivational elements for God to respond to the laments voiced by Zion are "the tragic reversal of the glory of Zion" and "Jerusalem's repentance," he elaborates only on the second of these and avers that "the admission of guilt and acceptance of responsibility for the calamity appears quite frequently." This claim is made despite the fact that the Zion figure mentions "sin" or "guilt" only twice (1:18, 22) and that her only statement of "repentance" (1:20) is textually very uncertain. But on the basis of this evidence, Ferris goes on to declare that Zion's "misbehavior" and "mishandling of her heritage" are the main points of the laments in chapters 1 and 2, thus effectively bracketing out the much more pervasive descriptions of pain and destruction.[21]

The repeated emphasis on the category of guilt that one finds among commentators is often linked to the category of hope. If admission of guilt represents a capitulation to God concerning responsibility for the destruction and the suffering it causes, then hope represents the reconciliation with God that follows on the heels of capitulation. Summarizing what he takes to be the major themes of Lamentations, Norman Gottwald writes:

> The steadfast insistence on God's righteousness and goodness declares itself in the conviction that as there has been a past glory and a present pain

there will be a future return marked by God's favor (3:31–36; 4:22; 5:21). Likewise the moment of the restoration of Israel's historical life begins when she has made full satisfaction for her guilt (4:11ab, 22ab). Then and only then will the tide of fortune turn in her direction . . . The future holds promise of restoration and therefore the basis for hope (3:20–36; 4:22; 5:21). Yahweh's lordship over history and its purposes are faithfully adhered to (3:31–36; 5:19). By these considerations the Book of Lamentations is imbued with greater significance than would be a mere lament.[22]

There are several significant points to be gleaned from this extended quotation. First, in order to sustain the linkage of hope with an admission of guilt, the author declines to make any reference to chapters 1 and 2; rather all references come from the latter chapters of Lamentations. Second, within these latter chapters there is a distinct emphasis on the central and more hopeful section of chapter 3, which gets mentioned three times. This is a characteristic move of interpreters: namely, to make claims about the major themes or theological intent of the book of Lamentations (note the use of such peremptory phrases as "steadfast insistence" and "conviction"), while drawing the support for their claims from a very circumscribed portion of text. Third, there is the assumption that what Gottwald calls "mere lament" is not a fitting religious disposition; something more than the language of lament is necessary in order to imbue the book of Lamentations with a "greater significance." Here again is a common strategy of interpreters: valuing lament only insofar as it leads to something that is less strident and mournful, and more conciliatory and hopeful. Otto Plöger writes, with no trace of irony: "In the poem of lament the feature of lamenting, regardless of how extensive it might be, has no importance in its own right."[23] Re'emi describes chapter 3 of Lamentations as "outstanding" and "superior in its artistry" to the other chapters, largely because the male figure "refuses to fall into the despair described at Lam. 2:20–22."[24] Rather: "Here we see how the poet turns from lament to prayer, to a new hope, where light comes into his darkness."[25] For Re'emi lament apparently cannot function as prayer. The fact that these interpreters move easily from description and analysis to explicit value judgments about the significance of lament and its status as religious discourse confirms that the bias toward capitulation and reconciliation is conditioned by theological presuppositions; it does not simply arise from the text itself.

The desire for an admission of guilt and the need for hope in the midst of even the most intense suffering come together in the emphasis on an attitude of submission, which then is presented as a model of behavior for readers both ancient and modern. Commenting on the transition from the first-person singular of the suffering man in the opening of chapter 3 to the first-person plural in 3:40, Mintz writes that "the appearance of the 'we' at this point implies that the recovery of the solidarity of community is contingent upon an awareness of sin and a commitment to a turning back to God."[26] Thus the behavior of the suffering man becomes the model for a recovered communal voice. Likewise, Hillers's "Everyman" is portrayed as a paragon of "patient faith and penitence, thus becoming a model for the nation."[27] For Brandscheidt, the model of the suffering man shows that lament is "a stance unbecoming for the truly pious."[28] Ewald, cited approvingly by Hillers, extols the virtues of the male figure insofar as he is able to "come to a proper recognition of his own sins and the necessity of repentance, and thereby to believing prayer." Ewald goes on to write:

> Who is this individual who thus laments, reflects and prays!—whose "I" unnoticed but at exactly the right point changes to "We"? O man, he is the image of your own self! Everyone should speak and think as he does. And so it comes about, unexpectedly, that just through this discourse which is most difficult at its beginning, for the first time pain is transformed into true prayer.[29]

More subtly, when Gottwald articulates what he calls the "theology of hope" found in Lamentations he writes that the book "inculcates" in its readers a "submissive spirit." Gottwald goes so far as to claim that "in Lamentations we come upon the most outspoken appeals for submission to be found anywhere in the Old Testament."[30] But all the examples he cites as support for such a far-reaching claim come from 3:25–33. Gottwald admits briefly that the figure of Zion does not quite fit this characterization, "for she is much more concerned with the bitterness of suffering and the pangs of sin," but in the same paragraph he nevertheless asserts that "an intimation of suffering that is purposeful is *the central teaching* of Lamentations, the axis around which all the confessing and lamenting revolves."[31] Such a central teaching can only be gleaned from chapter 3, for in chapters 1 and 2, and especially in those sections attributed to the figure of Zion, the notion that suffering may have a purpose is scarcely on the horizon.

The Figure of Zion as an Alternative Model

The three primary biases in modern interpretation of Lamentations identified above have worked together to ensure that readings, and especially *theological* readings, have focused on the male figure of chapter 3 to the exclusion of Zion. The Zion figure is quite obviously not male, does not lend itself to a typological Christian interpretation, and can hardly be characterized as modeling a submissive spirit toward suffering. Consequently, chapters 1 and 2 of Lamentations are given short shrift, are forced into the categories of guilt and hope whether they fit or not, or are simply denigrated as inferior to chapter 3. There are, however, a few notable exceptions to this tendency to focus on the suffering man among recent interpreters.

In his recent monograph on Lamentations, Claus Westermann argues emphatically against the tendency to ground theological interpretation only in chapter 3. He also weighs in against the tendency "to devalue the lament or to speak of it with depreciatory reserve."[32] Westermann asserts that the preference for chapter 3 is based on interpreters' desire to find explanations for suffering and models of proper behavior. However, according to Westermann, "[a]s a whole, Lamentations has neither an explanatory nor an admonitory function."[33] Westermann agrees with the majority of interpreters that the poet or poets of Lamentations view the destruction of Jerusalem as punishment for the sins of the nation, but he denies that this dictum is the primary drive behind the poetry. It is rather simply a given, and not something that the poetry is trying to inculcate in its readers. As an alternative to an explanatory or admonitory function, Westermann argues that "the real significance of laments resides in the way they allow the suffering of the afflicted to find expression."[34] He goes on to make a passionate plea for the importance of genuine lament language in the Christian Church, despite the fact that "the lament forces a confrontation with what is incomprehensible in the way God acts."[35] Throughout his excursus, "The Lament and Its Sig-

nificance," Westermann maintains a strong advocacy for the significance of lament language in its own right, thus conforming perhaps
more than any other contemporary interpreter to Adorno's axiom
linking truth to the willingness to let suffering speak.[36]

It is disappointing then to find that while Westermann has managed to break the hold of chapter 3 on contemporary interpretation
and attempt to reclaim the value of lament language, his own reading of chapters 1 and 2 is hardly less pious sounding and conciliatory
toward God than those of previous scholars. Though he has indicated that laments, even though they may acknowledge sin or guilt,
are not primarily concerned to convince readers or hearers of
such, Westermann works to convince his own readers of the importance of sin and guilt for Lamentations. In his treatment of chapter
1, Westermann attempts to demonstrate by reference to verses 5,
8–9, 14, and 18 "a special emphasis being placed on this motif of
acknowledgment of guilt."[37] He finds that verse 5 "specifies the
ultimate cause of this misery . . . All this misery has transpired because of Israel's guilt."[38] The reference to Jerusalem's sin in verse 8 is
labeled a "confession of sin" by Jerusalem, though it is not in fact
spoken by the Zion figure. And Westermann downplays the "accusation against God" (in form-critical terms, die Gott-Klage) of verses
12–17—assuring the reader that "the accusation against God which
lies before us here is not an actual indictment of God"—only to conclude that the section "receives its appropriate emphasis" in verse
18a, where Zion admits that God is in the right and that she has dis-
obeyed.[39] "Set over against the accusation against God," he writes,
"this [v. 18a] is a justification of all that God has done to Zion."[40]
When he moves to chapter 2 of Lamentations, Westermann has to
admit that the acknowledgment of guilt that he describes as running
"so clearly and unmistakably throughout Lam. 1" is much harder to
find. Conceding that it "appears to be lacking" altogether in chapter
2, Westermann nevertheless refers to guilt repeatedly in his comments. Though seemingly quite moved by the portrayal of children
dying in the streets—"The explanation that this was a divine punishment does not suffice, for what is the place of small children in
that!"[41]—he falls back on the standby interpretation: "These survivors directly experienced where the disobedience of the people finally led: to the incomprehensible suffering of the innocent, namely

the children." A similar extrapolation is found in his statement regarding the motif of wrath in 2:1–8, where he expected to find, but did not, an acknowledgment of guilt: "Where one finds passionately agitated speech about the wrath of Yahweh, present *by implication* is also reference to the cause of the divine wrath: Israel's guilt."[42] Thus in his comments on Lamentations 2, as with chapter 1, Westermann follows in the footsteps of virtually all modern interpreters by underscoring again and again the notion of guilt until it is raised to the status of a hermeneutical key, regardless of whether or not it even appears explicitly in the verses under consideration.

Westermann also follows in the footsteps of previous interpreters in his unremitting stress on the hope for reconciliation with God. As we saw with other interpreters above, Westermann links the hope for reconciliation with an admission of guilt. He asserts that one must read verses 1:9c and 1:11c—Zion's interruptive imperatives to God, "Look, O LORD"—as properly following and related to the supposed acknowledgment of guilt in verse 8a. "In order to grasp the connections here, one must first of all read this material without the lines interspersed in vv 8b–c, 10, and 11a–b."[43] This reading strategy, for which no justification is given, naturally encourages certain connections over others, especially the connection between guilt and the hope for divine intervention. And by emphasizing the continuity between the third-person description in verse 8 and the first-person speech of Zion, Westermann reinforces his construal of verse 8a as a confession of sin by Zion. Zion's unflinching imperatives for God to pay attention to her misery are reduced by Westermann to "the plea for God's gracious intervention."[44]

A similar theological toning-down occurs in Westermann's treatment of 2:18–19. The imperatives here are addressed to Zion:

> Cry out to the Lord from the heart,
> > wall of Daughter Zion.
> Shed tears like a torrent,
> > day and night!
> Give yourself no rest,
> > and do not let your eyes be still.
> Arise! Wail in the night,
> > at the beginning of every watch.
> Pour out your heart like water

> in front of the LORD.
> Lift your hands to him
>   for the lives of your children,
> who collapse from hunger
>   in the middle of the street.

Westermann comments on these verses: "In terms of their content, these imperatives more closely resemble the call to wait patiently upon Yahweh."[45] However one interprets these verses, and I will give my own interpretation in chapter two of this study, it is difficult to imagine them as constituting a call for patient waiting.

Two other recent interpreters have seen fit to challenge the pervasive emphasis on Lamentations 3 as the hermeneutical key that leads the reader to hope and reconciliation. In his commentary on Lamentations, Iain Provan argues that such an emphasis on the hopeful nature of the book "seems particularly misguided." "After many struggles," Provan writes, "it is doubt, not hope, with which the book leaves us; and to characterize Lamentations as a hopeful book is therefore to mislead."[46] For Provan, this is true even if one focuses solely on chapter 3.

> The central poem of the book does not, then, give us news of the triumph of faith over doubt, as has often been claimed by the commentators. It gives us only an interim report on a battle in progress.[47]

And while noting the presence of an "orthodox view of suffering" that admits of a causal relationship of sin and punishment, he also argues that such a view "does not seem so wholehearted," especially when one gets beyond the narrator's voice in the early verses of chapter 1.[48] Provan's commentary thus offers a much more even-handed treatment of chapters 1 and 2 in relation to chapter 3, and it allows for a more sympathetic view of Zion's "reproach of God" in 2:20–22.

The second recent scholar to focus on chapters 1 and 2 of Lamentations and to question the pervasiveness of the notion of guilt is F. W. Dobbs-Allsopp. Dobbs-Allsopp's important monograph, *Weep, O Daughter of Zion*, is a comparative study of the book of Lamentations and the Mesopotamian city-lament genre, the best known example of which is "The Lamentation over the Destruction of Ur." After a detailed comparison of Lamentations with the Mesopotamian city laments, Dobbs-Allsopp concludes that "Lamentations provides the best (and perhaps only) exemplar of an Israelite city lament in the Hebrew Bible."[49] While other genres—e.g., the communal lament, individual lament, and funeral dirge—may have contributed to the shaping of Lamentations, Dobbs-Allsopp finds that the city-lament genre is dominant among them.[50] Because Dobbs-Allsopp finds the most parallels with the Mesopotamian laments in chapters 1 and 2 of Lamentations (to a lesser degree in chapter 4, and hardly at all in chapters 3 and 5), his monograph becomes effectively a study of the Zion figure, as its title indicates. Consequently, the figure of Zion is given much more attention than is the case in the average commentary, and Dobbs-Allsopp finds in her "a vastly complex literary figure."[51] With regard to the question of sin and guilt, he follows Provan in asserting that while the themes are identifiably present, they should not be overemphasized. Indeed, for Dobbs-Allsopp "the sin motif is almost perfunctory in nature."[52]

Shifting the Focus of Research

The present study continues in the line of research begun by Westermann, Provan, and Dobbs-Allsopp. Like them I question the stress placed on the male figure of chapter 3, the importance of sin and guilt, and the ultimately hopeful nature of Lamentations. My own study will differ in obvious ways from their work, however. Westermann and Provan are constrained by the genre of commentary and so do not pursue the emphasis on chapters 1 and 2. Dobbs-Allsopp is constrained by the comparative method and so does not pursue the internal workings of Lamentations 1 and 2 or what the theological implications of these might be.[53] In this study, then, I intend to pursue the focus on the figure of Zion in chapters 1 and 2 of Lamentations, to articulate the internal workings of the chapters (i.e., the rhetorical force they exert on readers), and to show how just such a focus and articulation are warranted by the history of precritical Jewish interpretation (that is, interpretations that predate the rise of modern biblical scholarship). I present this history of precritical interpretation as a subject worthy of study in and of itself, but also as an alternative to the critical insistence that chapter 3 should be the preeminent object of study in Lamentations and that it alone should serve as the basis of theological appropriation of the book.

By focusing on Lamentations 1 and 2, I have necessarily given less

attention to chapters 4 and 5. This is not due to a judgment that they
are unworthy of study or inferior in some way to the rest of the book,
but rather is dependent on several practical considerations. My focus
is on the figure of Zion as an alternative to the suffering man of chapter 3. While I would agree with the critical consensus that all five
chapters likely existed separately before being gathered together as
the book of Lamentations, chapters 1 and 2 are linked by the personification of the city of Zion as a woman; this does not take place
in any of the other chapters. The placing of these two chapters together, whether intentional or not, allows for a continuous reading
from one to the other, which is exactly how precritical readers would
have approached the text. And because a very large part of this study
deals with the history of interpretation, my focus is conditioned to
a certain degree by that history, which as I will show below has paid
a great deal of attention to Lamentations 1 and 2.

The title of this study is *Surviving Lamentations*. I use the term "survival" in a number of ways. First, as this introductory chapter has indicated, it is my judgment that readers of Lamentations are forced to
come up with strategies for surviving the book's harsh and violent, as
well as theologically challenging, images and language. Second, I read
chapters 1 and 2 of Lamentations as "literature of survival," that is, literature produced in the aftermath of a major catastrophe and its ac-
companying atrocities by survivors of that catastrophe. Arguing
against the idea that one should attempt to find a "spiritual process"
or "conceptual undertaking" in Lamentations, Westermann presents
a provocative but brief aside: "The issue in this text is one of survival
as such."[54] I pursue this hint with reference to twentieth-century literature of survival, which I find to be a compellingly appropriate way
to make the book of Lamentations relevant to contemporary readers.
Third, in my treatment of the literary character of Zion, I argue that a
concern for the survival of her children plays a privileged and critical
role. It is survival, rather than the theological categories of guilt or
hope, that I take to be a sort of hermeneutical key to the poetry of
chapters 1 and 2. Finally, I construe those texts in the history of interpretation that have also identified the fate of the children of Zion
as of primary concern as "survivals" of Lamentations, in the sense
that they represent an afterlife for the biblical book, not only drawing
their own life from it but allowing it to live on in later generations.

ONE

Matters of Life and Death:
Literature of Survival and the
Survival of Literature

I want to go on living even after my death.

Anne Frank

What must we do to allow a text to live?

Jacques Derrida

Anne Frank was a flesh-and-blood girl who died in the Nazi concentration camp of Bergen-Belsen in March of 1945. She did not survive. Jacques Derrida is a philosopher writing in the epigraph above about the survival of texts, the way in which a text may go on living in and through other texts. Surely the two cannot be talking of the same "survival." Surely not; the issues of survival that arise when one considers the situation of Anne Frank cannot be conflated with Derrida's use of survival as a theoretical term. Yet if these senses of survival are not entirely the same, neither are they entirely different. For the young girl is also a philosopher, who connects her notion of survival with writing. Referring to a fairy tale that she is trying to write, Anne Frank laments that "in my mind I know exactly how to go on, but somehow it doesn't flow from my pen."

> Perhaps I shall never finish it, it may land up in the wastepaper basket, or the fire . . . that's a horrible idea, but then I think to myself, "At the age of fourteen and with so little experience, how can you write about philosophy?"[1]

The philosopher Derrida also knows that the "death of the author" (a common metaphor among literary theorists) can in fact be taken quite literally. Remarking on the "unfinishedness" of Percy Bysshe

Shelley's poem, *The Triumph of Life* (on which Shelley was working when he died by drowning), Derrida asks: "Where are we to situate the event of Shelley's drowning? And who will decide the answer to this question? Who will form a narrative of these borderline events? At whose demand?"[2]

Like the epigraphs from Anne Frank and Jacques Derrida, my study of survival and the book of Lamentations recognizes the multiple meanings of the term "survival." On the one hand, it works from a recognition that Lamentations may be understood as a *literature of survival*, in the most basic sense of having been written in the aftermath of the physical destruction of Jerusalem and the death or survival of its flesh-and-blood inhabitants. In this sense of the term "survival," the biblical book may be usefully compared with modern literature of survival. The content of the book itself calls attention to issues of survival in the face of destruction, as the survival of her children becomes an overriding concern of personified Zion. Since the children of Zion are poetic representations of the inhabitants of the city of Jerusalem, this concern for the survival of children reflects as well a larger concern for the survival of the Jewish people. Thus, the concern over the threat to children that is so prominent in Lamentations, while in all likelihood rooted in the genuine experience of the survival of the destruction of cities in the ancient Near East, refers also to the concern for the future of a people.

On the other hand, my study is concerned not only with how Lamentations relates to the literature of survival, but also how it relates to the *survival of literature*. This is not double talk or mere semantics. My invoking of Anne Frank relates primarily to the first of these, while my invoking of Jacques Derrida relates primarily to the second, in which survival functions as a metaphor for how a text generates other texts, thereby "living on" beyond what might be its expected life span. But as was the case with the quotes from Anne Frank and Derrida, these two uses of survival are mutually implicated. For as this study will argue, Lamentations' existence as a literature of survival drives its survival as literature in later texts.

Literature of Survival

The fundamental fact of any literature of survival is that something or someone "that is dead or ought to be, is still alive."[3] The paradox: death in life, life in death. The two are not so absolutely separable. One could argue, of course, that in the midst of all life there is death, both the experienced death of others and the threat of one's own death. But a literature of survival has a more thoroughgoing alliance to this paradox. It is more keenly aware of the facts of life and the facts of death. Though necessarily written from the perspective of one who has lived through or lived beyond, for the time being, the events it attempts to convey, such literature is all too often only a step ahead of the death of the author. When the author does manage to live beyond the death he or she describes, it is only by some "illicit grace," to borrow a phrase from George Steiner, that remains forever unsettling. Conversely, when one is aware that the author has not survived, as in the well-known case of Anne Frank, a reader may have the fleeting experience of allowing the author to live again, if only until the book is closed and replaced on its shelf.

In its embodiment of paradox, the literature of survival works to keep alive the memory of death. When it has accomplished its work, it forces an awareness of the constancy of death on its readers as well. Texts of survival, then, at least those that have survived, reach out beyond themselves. Survivors speak and write and fix the memory of death not just as a monument to those who died or as a record of events ensuring that the world never forgets, as important as these tasks are for the literature. The literature of survival has a more active concern as well: to recruit the reader or hearer, to sway its audience away from neutrality and toward the concerns of the survivor. In the preface to his memoir, *Survival in Auschwitz*, Primo Levi writes:

> The need to tell our story to "the rest," to make "the rest" participate in it, had taken on for us, before our liberation and after, the character of an immediate and violent impulse, to the point of competing with our other elementary needs.[4]

Likewise, Jean Améry prefaces his book, *At the Mind's Limits: Contemplations by a Survivor on Auschwitz and Its Realities*, with the following statement:

> To the extent that the reader would venture to join me at all he will have no choice but to accompany me, in the same tempo, through the same darkness that I illuminated step by step.[5]

In his influential study of both Nazi and Stalinist concentration camps, *The Survivor: An Anatomy of Life in the Death Camps*, Terrence Des Pres has described this rhetorical aim of the survivor:

> In the literature of survival we find an image of things so grim, so heart-breaking, so starkly unbearable, that inevitably the survivor's scream begins to be our own. When this happens the role of the spectator is no longer enough.[6]

One might be justifiably skeptical about the inevitability of the success of this rhetorical gambit. It is too easy to imagine readers and hearers not being swayed by the testimony. For one reason or another the work of the literature of survival might go unaccomplished, the audience might not be swayed, the scream might simply die out. The "I" of the survivor addresses a "you" that it desperately strives to bring into conversation, to goad into responding. Yet the very intensity of its rhetoric witnesses to the fact that the literature of survival is all too aware that it might well fail.

Before going further it is necessary to define, to the extent possible, what is meant by the term "survival" and the phrase "literature of survival." *Webster's Ninth New Collegiate Dictionary* defines "survival" as "a living beyond the life of or continuing longer than another person, thing or event." To "survive" is defined quite simply as "to remain alive or in existence." Such unadorned definitions are useful for identifying the commonality among the various uses to which the concept of survival will be put in the pages that follow. Yet as Lawrence Langer rightly points out, one must keep in mind that there are in fact different *versions* of survival.[7]

The unadorned definitions of survival quickly become adorned. Des Pres defines survival as "the capacity of men and women to live beneath the pressure of protracted crisis, to sustain terrible damage in mind and body and yet be there, sane, alive, still human."[8] Des Pres's version of survival, though taking account of "the terrible damage sustained," focuses on the capacity to live in spite of this, on the persistence of "life itself."[9] By contrast, in his study of survivors of the atomic bomb dropped on Hiroshima in World War II, Robert Jay Lifton informs the reader that the most common Japanese word for survivor, *seizonsha*, is rarely used in Japan to refer to those who lived through the bomb.[10] The term is thought to overemphasize the "idea of being alive." Two other terms are used instead: *hibakusha*, meaning "explosion-affected person," and *higaisha*, meaning "victim or injured party." The emphasis shifts with these terms from the experience of remaining alive to the experience of that which one has lived through. Lawrence Langer's treatment of survival also reflects this shift, arguing that the traditional opposition between "living and dying" must give way in the twentieth century to "a more complex relationship between survival and atrocity."

> "Living" opens out into the future, governed by the expectation of fulfillment; "survival" draws its energy from the past, and is burdened by unforgettable memories that offer little relief to the individual simply because he has survived them.[11]

For Langer, the concept of survival arising out of the Nazi Holocaust must focus, in a way similar to the Japanese avoidance of the term *seizonsha*, on the experiences of suffering and death rather than the experience of continued life.

These versions of survival exist within a growing body of works that I will refer to as twentieth-century "literature of survival." By this I mean both works by survivors themselves and the secondary works that attempt to analyze the experience of survival. Often this distinction is impossible to maintain; for while many survivors are content to try to relate their experiences (for example, Elie Wiesel's *Night*, Primo Levi's *Survival in Auschwitz*, and Charlotte Delbo's *Auschwitz and After*), others are engaged in a more explicit task of analysis (for example, Jean Améry's *At the Mind's Limits*, Bruno Bettelheim's *The Informed Heart*, and Victor Frankl's *Man's Search for Meaning*). As this list of works indicates, for the most part I have limited myself, within the larger category of twentieth-century survival literature, to works relating to the Holocaust.[12] To undertake a comparative study of the various literatures of survival—which might include in its purview the Armenian massacres, the firebombing of Dresden, the Stalinist purges of the U.S.S.R., the Chinese cultural revolution, the Indonesian mass murder of communists, etc. (the list is potentially endless, right up to current events in Rwanda and the former Yugoslavia)—is, for obvious reasons involving limitations of space and my own scholarly competence, impossible. In addition to such practical considerations, however, the Holocaust as an event in Jewish history is directly related to my study of the history of Jewish interpretation of the book of Lamentations.

Even within the more circumscribed realm of Holocaust literature, however, one must adjudicate between differing versions of survival. Those of Frankl, Bettelheim, and Lifton and Olson emphasize the purposiveness of suffering and the persistence of hope. Regarding those fellow concentration camp prisoners who he thought "overlooked the opportunities to make something positive of camp life," Frankl writes: "Such people forgot that often it is just such an exceptionally difficult external situation which gives man the opportunity to grow spiritually."[13] For Frankl, "[s]uffering ceases to be suffering the moment it finds a meaning."[14] To this notion of the purposiveness of suffering, Bettelheim adds the concept of guilt, writing that the moral growth resulting from suffering includes not only "understanding" and "compassion," but also "the ability to feel guilty."[15] Likewise, Lifton and Olson wax poetic about "the suffering which prepares the way for the deepest insight and the greatest ecstasy," comparing it to "the winter which makes possible spring, the dark of night followed by the light of day."[16] It is clear that in the version of survival presented by these writers it is intolerable that suffering might exist outside a framework of meaning, and that it is up to the literature of survival to make such meaning manifest.

The versions of survival presented by Améry, Des Pres, and Langer, by contrast, emphasize the fact of suffering itself, arguing that such suffering exists outside structures of meaning and may in fact work to subvert the making of meaning altogether. At the very least, for these writers, suffering and survival call into question romantic notions of a "good death," death as a wellspring for art, or a heroic stoicism in the face of atrocity. Améry writes: "For death in its literary, philosophic, or musical form there was no place in Auschwitz. No bridge led from death in Auschwitz to *Death in Venice*."[17] Des Pres, though finally opting to focus on "the thrust of life itself, a strength beyond hope, as stubborn as the upsurge of spring,"[18] does so only after an unflinching presentation of the gas chambers, the torture, the threat of freezing, and the "excremental assault" of dysentery. More than anyone else, perhaps, Lawrence Langer resists the imposition of sense or purpose on the suffering and death, and the survival, represented by the Holocaust. For

Langer, suffering has no redeeming purpose and gives no tragic insight, death represents no heroic sacrifice or symbolic closure, and survival is not a rebirth, renewal, or triumph of the human spirit. The function of survival literature is not to divine the purpose or meaning of either death or survival; nor should it make great pronouncements concerning human dignity. Rather, the Holocaust represents "a revelation of moral chaos,"[19] and survival is a matter of chance and the vicissitudes of camp life. The testimony of survivors is thus not so much about "a talent for life" (as Des Pres puts it) as it is an "homage to the dead."[20]

My own version of survival—that is, my appropriation of twentieth-century literature of survival as a means for rereading Lamentations—is indebted to this second group of writers much more than the first. Unlike Frankl, Bettelheim, and Lifton and Olson, who all tend to begin and end within the realm of abstraction and explanation, Améry, Des Pres, and Langer (as well as writers such as Elie Wiesel, Nelly Sachs, and Charlotte Delbo) insist that one face squarely the realities of suffering and death before one attempts to interpret survival. Such an insistence will serve well to balance the tendency of modern biblical scholars to downplay or denigrate descriptions of pain and suffering in their treatments of Lamentations in favor of theological categories of sin and guilt.

Survival of Literature

Surviving Lamentations is not only about reading Lamentations in relation to literature of survival, but also in relation to the survival of literature. While these are two distinct tasks, there is a significant amount of overlap conditioned by the centrality of the concept of survival for each. This overlap will be clear in the following exposition of the two main theoreticians of the survival of literature to be treated in this section: Walter Benjamin and Jacques Derrida.

Walter Benjamin and the Task of Translation

My explication of the survival of literature begins with Walter Benjamin's essay from 1923, "The Task of the Translator."[21] Many commentators have noted the difficulty of reading this notoriously, but richly, intricate introduction to a translation of Baudelaire's Tableaux parisiens. Susan Handelman notes that it has been read in "any num-

ber of contradictory ways."[22] Paul de Man writes: "Whenever I go
back to this text, I think I have it more or less, then I read it again,
and again I don't understand it."[23] The essay has been taken as an
early example of "reception theory," as well as a denial of the legiti-
macy of such theory. It has been taken as a statement of the theological basis for the ultimate unity of all languages, as well as a denial
that such unity can ever exist. My purpose here is not to adjudicate
between these various claims, but to focus in on Benjamin's central
metaphor for translation, that is, "survival," which in more recent
years has been picked up and expanded by Jacques Derrida.[24]

Benjamin begins with a characteristically programmatic statement, which he then proceeds to make more problematic and more
complex throughout the essay: "No poem is intended for the reader,
no picture for the beholder, no symphony for the listener."[25] But this
statement should not be read as an assertion, à la New Criticism, of
a work's essential completeness in and of itself. In fact, Benjamin is
little concerned in the essay with the nature of the work of art in and
of itself. He is rather concerned to explore the relationship between
the original work of art and its reproducibility, or in the case of the
literary work, its translatability. It is helpful at this point to note that
Benjamin separates a work's "subject matter" from its "truth content." To say that a poem or symphony is intended for the reader or
the listener would be to focus on the subject matter, or on the com-
municative aspect of the work of art, its "imparting of information."
Benjamin focuses instead, with obvious mystical overtones, on "the
unfathomable, the mysterious, the 'poetic,'" toward which works of
art strive.[26] This is not to say that the reader or the hearer or the
viewer cannot also be aware of this striving even as he or she participates in the communication of sense or appreciates the subject matter that serves as the more mundane vehicle for the mysterious tenor,
but only that the work of art is unconcerned with whether this is the
case or not. Elsewhere, in an essay on Goethe's Elective Affinities, Benjamin admits that the subject matter and the truth content of a work
of art are intimately bound up "at the beginning of a work's history."[27] It is in the work's "afterlife" that the two become separate
and able to be separately evaluated. Evaluating the subject matter of
the work is the job of the commentator, while evaluating the truth
content of the work is the job of the critic. Comparing the respective

tasks of the commentator and the critic to those of the chemist and the alchemist considering fire, Benjamin notes that the chemist is occupied with analyzing "wood and ashes," while the alchemist is occupied with "the enigma of the flame itself." "Thus, the critic inquires into the truth, whose living flame continues to burn over the heavy logs of what is past and the light ashes of life gone by."[28]

In "The Task of the Translator," it is to this "afterlife" that Benjamin turns his attention, and in doing so pursues further the "vital connection"[29] between original works and their reproductions or translations, that is, he construes this relationship as one between the life of a work and its afterlife. If an original work of literary art is unconcerned with imparting information to the reader, then it follows for Benjamin that a translation is similarly unconcerned for its reader. The hallmark of a "bad translation" is that it tries to convey the same information that the original conveyed to its reader. But if translations do not exist for the sake of the readers into whose language they are translated, for what or whom do they exist? For the sake of the original itself. Benjamin's claim is that a "good translation" is not born in order to make the original available for later readers, though it may in fact do that, but rather because the original "calls for" (71) its own translation. The work demands translation because there is something in the original that can live on only in translation. Benjamin is not so naive as to believe that the demand will always be met, however, for although he contends that translatability is an essential feature of certain works, "it is not to say that it is essential that they be translated." Works may well go untranslated, and in such a case what is lost is "a specific significance inherent in the original" that "manifests itself in its translatability."[30]

In explicating this relationship between original and translation—one in which the original calls for and requires a translation, but is not itself affected by or even "aware" of the translation(s) it engenders—Benjamin makes his clearest statement about the vitalist connection.

> Just as the manifestations of life are intimately connected with life itself without signifying anything for it, a translation issues from the original—not so much from its life as from its "afterlife." For a translation comes after the original and for the important works, which never find their chosen translator at the time of their birth, is a stage of continued life.[31]

A translation, then, both participates in the survival of a text (its afterlife) and ensures its survival (or continued life) in succeeding
generations. Thus a translation both owes its life to the original and
functions to preserve the original's life. But Benjamin makes clear
that it is not the *purpose* of the translation to serve the work, but rather
to engage in the same striving toward the unfathomable. There is the
implication in Benjamin's treatment that the original is always
doomed to fall short in this striving, and that because of this lack
"the work reflects the great longing for linguistic complementa-
tion."[32] The translation survives the original because the original has
failed in the task it has set itself. But it is in its very failing that its survival in translation is ensured: if the task of the original had been
met, there would be no call for translation. What is this mysterious
task? What is it that the original inevitably fails to achieve? It is, paradoxically, its translatability, "the translation of translation" as Derrida puts it. Because Benjamin sees the ultimate goal of linguistic creation as attaining to the realm of "pure language,"[33] and because no
individual language can attain that goal on its own, the "essential"
quality of a linguistic work of art is to give birth to other works of
art (in this case translations) that might supplement its striving toward this goal. The "task of the translator" is not to make the original clear to those speakers of the translator's language, but rather to
"release in his own language that pure language which is under the
spell of another, to liberate the language imprisoned in a work in his
re-creation of that work."[34] Benjamin is approaching, if not entering,
the realm of mysticism. Indeed, he seems to implicitly indicate his
awareness of this fact in his assertion that "both the original and the
translation [are] recognizable as fragments of a greater language, just
as fragments are part of a vessel."[35] For no doubt somewhere behind
this metaphor, especially given Benjamin's close association with the
well-known scholar of Jewish mysticism Gershom Scholem, lies the
kabbalistic notion of "the breaking of the vessels" (*shevirat ha-kelim*),
according to which the flow of divine life proved too much for the
primordial vessels that were to contain it and shattered them, scat-
tering the fragments (each containing a divine spark) throughout
creation. The goal of humanity in general and the mystic in particular is to work to reunite these fragments and restore the broken vessels.[36] But it is important to note that for Benjamin the "original"

work is not the vessel that is then completed by the translation (contra, for example, John Lechte),[37] but that both are necessary fragments of another vessel: the pure language toward which they strive. So there is no sense that the demand for translation, for the survival of a work, will ever finally be met once and for all.

Jacques Derrida and the Triumph of Life

In his recent article, "Des Tours de Babel," Jacques Derrida has engaged at length Benjamin's articulation of survival as a metaphor for translation. While I will come back in chapter three to that article, here I will consider Derrida's earlier essay "Living On: Borderlines." Though Benjamin is nowhere mentioned in the text of the essay, he no doubt inhabits its pretext, for here Derrida treats the two subjects most germane to "The Task of the Translator": translation, and the survival of literature. Derrida's text is split horizontally into two sections, with the upper section (entitled "Living On") exploring "the complex senses of survival or living on of literature,"[38] and the bottom section (entitled "Borderlines") serving ostensibly as a running note to the translator of his essay, which was in fact written for translation, that is, it was originally published in English rather than in Derrida's native French.

The occasion for the writing of "Living On: Borderlines" was a commissioned volume, Deconstruction and Criticism, that was intended to showcase the "method" or project of what had become known in the 1970s as the "Yale School" of criticism. The volume included chapters by Harold Bloom, Paul de Man, Derrida, Geoffrey Hartman, and J. Hillis Miller. The agreed-upon common denominator of all the chapters was to be a consideration, to at least some degree, of Percy Bysshe Shelley's epic poem, The Triumph of Life. Derrida never really makes it past the title of the poem, however, using the phrase "the triumph of life" as a way not into the poem, but into his discussion of the trope of "survival." His discussion makes clear that this is no whim of deconstructive freeplay that chooses to treat whatever unrelated topic comes to mind; rather the dynamics of survival are inscribed already in the title, The Triumph of Life, and in the knowledge that Shelley died before completing the poem.

Derrida, aware of the fact that he is writing in French a text that is to have its first life in English, notes that the very syntax of the French phrase triomphe-de contains a double affirmation of "triumph of and triumph *over*" life.[39] Thus the English translator of Derrida's essay must choose how to render this phrase each time it occurs. Does it indicate an unambiguous sense of life triumphing over death, or is there also a sense of life triumphed over by death? With great poignancy, Derrida connects this double sense of the triumph of life with the actual death of Shelley:

> I maintain, not without delaying the proof a bit longer, that this is a question of what takes place in the poem and of what remains of it, beyond any opposition between finished and unfinished, whether we mean the end of the last poem or that of the man who drowned "off Lerici" on 8 July 1822, "writing *The Triumph of Life.*"[40]

Though Shelley does not survive, his poem does. Once the reader knows this biographical fact, this reason for the poem's "unfinishedness," it cannot but color the reading of the poem's title. And even if one does not have access to the double meaning of the French phrase, one can feel the irony of an author "writing the triumph of life" on the edge of his own death, particularly when one "finishes" or completes the poem with reference to all of Shelley's death knells: "On Death," "Death," "Autumn: A Dirge," and the fragment "The Death Knell Is Ringing."[41]

This basic ambiguity of survival pervades Derrida's whole treatment of the survival of literature. Survival, he writes, "is neither life nor death, but rather LIVING ON, the very progression of life and death. Living on is not the opposite of living, just as it is not identical with living."[42] Derrida underscores this fundamental ambiguity of survival by pairing up *The Triumph of Life* with a novella by Maurice Blanchot, *L'arrêt de mort.* What the two works share is exactly this ambiguity, indicated right away in their titles. Just as Derrida teased out a double meaning in *triomphe de,* so too he oscillates between the "death sentence" that seems to be the first-level meaning of the title for the Blanchot novella and the "suspension of death" that the title may also carry. For the *arrêt* may be taken as a "sentence" or "decision" at the same time as a "suspension" or "stoppage." Derrida's explication of survival, then, participates in a blurring of borders, an overlap, between life and death that is positively manifested in the life that wells up in the midst of death but negatively manifested in the infiltration of death into life.

[L]iving on goes beyond both living and dying, supplementing each
with a sudden surge and a certain reprieve, deciding [arrêtant] life and
death, ending them in a decisive arrêt, the arrêt that puts an end to something and the arrêt that condemns with a sentence [sentence], a statement, a
spoken word or a word that goes on speaking.[43]

Derrida thus mines these two works of literature in his attempt to articulate the paradoxical dynamic of survival: death in the midst of life,
life beyond the borders of death. Or as Jean-François Lyotard has succinctly put it, "The word survivor implies that an entity that is dead
or ought to be is still alive."[44] Survival is a persistent "thereness" of
some thing that ought not to be there, a continuance of being in the
face of nothingness. In his study of survival in concentration camps,
Des Pres writes that "[g]hetto and camp regulations were designed to
make life impossible."[45] In a world designed to make life impossible,
it nevertheless persists, but ever precariously. Des Pres, in the very
next line, makes an unwitting wordplay that further drives home Derrida's point when he states that "survival" was possible only because
of an "underworld" of illegal activities. The "overlife" (sur-vival) is
dependent on the "underworld" (the traditional place of death).

How do these reflections on the general nature of survival relate
more specifically to the survival of literature? Typically, Derrida does
not provide the reader of his essay with a program for applying his
notion of survival to texts. What he does instead is to provide a rich
and complex web of rumination and allusion, constructed from repeated etymological musings on survival (both the French survie and
the German Überleben), as well as his conscription of The Triumph of Life
and L'arrêt de mort, the latter concerning a woman "who was dead" yet
nonetheless "returned to life."[46] Many of the etymological senses
that Derrida extracts from "survival" depend on the prefix "sur": "super, hyper, 'over,' über, and even 'above' and 'beyond.'"[47] In light of the
polysemous nature of the "sur," survival may take on the following diverse senses: "a reprieve or an afterlife, 'life after life' or life after
death, more life or more than life, and better."[48] In the "Borderlines"
section of the essay, the running note to the translators, Derrida does
make a more or less explicit allusion to how survival relates to
translation, echoing Benjamin, when he writes that, "The sur, 'on,'
'super-,' and so forth, that is my theme above, also designates the
figure of a passage by trans-lation, the trans- of an Übersetzung."[49]

A discussion more germane to how texts may be said to "survive" is to be found in the section of the essay that focuses on the question of defining the borders or edges of a text.[50] In this section one finds a familiar example of what has become known as Derridean "deconstruction." He begins, in a manner similar to his treatment of the "preface" in *Dissemination*, by asking the seemingly naive question of how one decides when a text begins or ends.[51] To approach (*aborder*) a text, there must be some edge or border (*bord*) to it. Is the title the upper border to the text? Or is the border constituted by the first line after the title? Or what if one begins reading somewhere after the first line? Does that point then become the edge of the text? And is the lower edge of the text simply that point at which the ink stops? What if the work breaks off, is "unfinished" in the sense that Shelley's poem was unfinished, "at the moment when, in greatest proximity to the signature, at the apparent lower edge of the poem, the signatory is drowned, loses his footing, loses sight of the shore (*bord de mer*)"?[52] Derrida complicates the matter by bringing in the example of a text that "quotes and requotes, with or without quotation marks."[53] Is the border of this text stable? Does it not give way to include those texts from which it quotes? Given the belated nature of language, that it always comes to us having been used elsewhere, such quotation "with or without quotation marks" must always be taking place. So from his initial question about the edge of a text, Derrida calls into question the very notion of a stable border that might separate one text from another. He imagines instead:

> [a] "text" that is henceforth no longer a finished corpus of writing, some content enclosed in a book or its margins, but a differential network, a fabric of traces referring endlessly to something other than itself, to other differential traces. Thus the text overruns all the limits assigned to it so far (not submerging or drowning them in an undifferentiated homogeneity, but rather making them more complex, dividing and multiplying strokes and lines).[54]

This is familiar poststructuralist ground, but what is not so familiar is to consider this manifesto of intertextuality in relation to survival.

For Derrida, the survival of texts, the survival of literature, depends on this overrun (*de-bordement*). The triumph of life takes place "at the edge of death," and survival takes place at the edge of the text. This triumph over death, to take place at all, "must be excessive."[55] The survival of a literary work takes place when the work overruns its borders, breaks through the dams that have been erected against it, and makes its presence felt in other works, "with or without quotation marks." *Survivre*, Derrida avers, is "not *living* or (not living) *maintaining oneself*, lifeless, in a pure state of supplement," but is rather "stopping [*arrêter*] the dying, a stopping [*arrêt*] that does not stop it, that on the contrary makes it go on, makes it last [*durer*]."[56] To imagine a text existing complete in and of itself is to imagine not "survival" but a "lifeless" state of preservation. Paradoxically, the "unfinished edge" of the text, its point of dying out, its "*arrêt de mort*," allows it to go on, to endure, by calling other texts that respond to it. It is the unfinished edge's refusal to be finished that converts the death sentence to a suspension of death.

The Precariousness of Survival

Looking ahead to the book of Lamentations, and borrowing from Derrida, I submit that "its unfinishedness is structural; it is bound to itself in the shifting binding of the *arrêt*."[57] The response that Zion demands from God concerning the survival of her children never comes. The death sentence pronounced over the children seems to have the final word. But in those works that survive Lamentations, it is precisely this intolerable death sentence that is converted into a suspension of death and into life in excess. It is important to recognize, as Derrida does in the quote above, that this textual *de-bordement* does not refer to an "undifferentiated homogeneity,"[58] in which all texts everywhere are equally related and all borders are indeterminate. It is, after all, impossible to read all texts everywhere at the same time.[59] The *de-bordement* refers instead to that discrete moment—when one's reading is arrested, when one approaches (*aborder*) and indeed goes over the unfinished edge—when the reader responds to the demand of the text by taking up (*aborder*) another text, or by taking up a pen and writing another text. Derrida illustrates this moment with reference to Blanchot's *L'arrêt de mort*, which is structured as two separate narratives (*récits*) between which lies a blank space.

> Within this framework, the strange construction of the double narrative
> is held together at an invisible hinge, a double inner edge [*bord*] (the space
> between the last sentence of the first *recit* and the first of the second).[60]

This blank space—the space that separates a death sentence from a
suspension of death—is all-important. "The truth beyond truth of
living on: the middle of the *récit*, its element, its ridge, its backbone
[*arête*]."[61] Between the *arrêt de mort* as death sentence and the *arrêt de mort*
as suspension of death lies the *arête*, the backbone that supports both
equally, the ridge from which one can look in either direction.

It is also important to recognize then that safe passage from one
side of the *arête* to the other is not guaranteed. As Benjamin admitted
that the demand for translation can remain a demand even when it
is not met, so too one must admit that the demand for survival no
more guarantees an afterlife than "the agony of the starving assures
them of food."[62] In between Lamentations and those texts that survive it lies the blank space, the border that threatens to deny passage,
the possibility of closing the book of life.

TWO

"None Survived or Escaped": Reading for Survival in Lamentations 1 and 2

In my happier days I used to remark on the aptitude of the saying, "When in life we are in the midst of death." I have since learnt that it's more apt to say, "When in death we are in the midst of life."

A survivor of the Belsen concentration camp

There are two kinds of discoveries in literary matters: the work that is complete in its very incompletion—an incompletion ineluctably carried to term—and the work that has come only halfway toward its always deferred completion.

Edmond Jabès

To read for survival in Lamentations 1 and 2, in terms of the version of survival that I describe in chapter one, would mean attending to those elements of the poems that represent the paradox of death in the midst of life and life beyond the borders of death, the expression of pain for its own sake, and the way in which the rhetoric of the poetry is concerned to move beyond description to persuasion. In doing just this in what follows, I argue that survival is inscribed in the biblical text of Lamentations in the larger design of the chapters as well as in the details of their content.

Life and Death in Lamentations 1 and 2

Biblical critics have had a difficult time settling on the technical genre of these two poems. One finds them identified variously as communal laments (*Klagelieder des Volkes*), individual laments (*Klagelieder des Einzelnen*), and dirges (*Leichenlieder* or *Totenklagen*), all of which genres are related but distinct. The initial form-critical designation of these chapters (along with Lamentations 4) as dirges in a classic work by Hermann Gunkel and Joachim Begrich has dominated the critical discussion.[1] According to this line of thinking they are funeral songs; but instead of referring to a dead individual they refer to the death of a nation.[2] Hedwig Jahnow's 1923 study, *Das hebräische Leichenlied* (The Hebrew dirge), explores in more depth the genre of the dirge, or funeral song, within the context of world folk literature. She concludes that certain elements of the dirge are identifiable in Lamentations 1 and 2: the opening mournful cry ("Alas" or "How"; איכה), the summons to weep, and the description of the mourner's suffering. One very important element is missing however: the announcement that someone has died. Moreover, there are elements in these chapters that do not show up in dirges, including "the summoning of Yahweh, the lamenting over the distress, the plea for Yahweh to take notice, the confession of guilt."[3] Jahnow concludes that these elements are borrowed from the "popular psalms of lamentation" in the service of "the transformation of an originally entirely profane type into a religious poem."[4] For Jahnow, Lamentations 1 and 2 are understood primarily as dirges that have borrowed motifs from the psalms of lament in order to make a theological statement about the death they describe.

Since these programmatic studies, scholars have tried in differing ways to account for the slippage in genre one finds in these poems. Most often it is decided, either explicitly or implicitly, that they represent what Gunkel and Begrich called mixed types (or *Mischungen*).[5] Otto Eissfeldt writes:

> Poems 1, 2, and 4 are, as their opening word איכה, Ah, how! shows, funeral dirges and in fact political funeral dirges in which it is a political entity, Jerusalem, which is lamented over as dead . . . But in none of them does the type appear in its pure form.[6]

Eissfeldt goes on to separate the genres in chapter 1 by verse, finding that while 1:1–11 and 17 belong primarily to the genre of dirge, verses 9c, 11c, and 12–16 are completely in the style of the individual song of lamentation. Chapter 2 he identifies as a dirge, though in this case he does not attempt to deal with any divergence from the genre that the chapter may contain. Claus Westermann has devoted much energy to the form-critical analysis of Lamentations, coming to an essentially converse conclusion to that of Jahnow. With regard to chapter 1, he writes:

> So the judgment of Jahnow—viz., that with regard to its structure Lam 1 is a dirge into which several motifs of the communal lament have been incorporated—must be rejected. Rather, in Lam 1 the structure of the communal lament can quite clearly be discerned. It is into the latter's structure that isolated elements of the dirge have been inserted.[7]

Chapter 2, for Westermann, belongs nearly exclusively to the category of communal lament: "Only the mournful cry at the beginning really belongs to the dirge."[8] Other interpreters agree with Westermann on the mixture of dirge and lament, yet identify the lament as that of an individual rather than a community.[9] Gottwald takes a synthetic approach, writing that "[b]oth the funeral song and the individual lament as formal types are employed here and there, but always in the communal sense."[10]

It is clear that we have in chapters 1 and 2 of Lamentations a certain mixture or combination of genres: the more common lament (whether understood as individual or communal) and the dirge or funeral song. What is less clear, and what I will argue now, is that the combination of the genres is not haphazard or confused. Rather it evinces the fundamental dynamic of survival literature identified above: the paradox of life in death and death in life.

It is apparent that when scholars have attempted to separate the genres in chapter 1, they have tended to do so along the lines established by the change in speaker between Zion and the poet.[11] The voice of the poet holds sway for nearly all of the first half of chapter 1 (vv. 1–11) and proceeds in dirgelike fashion to describe the ruination of Zion, personified as a woman.[12] Particularly characteristic of the dirge are the following elements: the opening exclamatory "Alas" or "How" (in Hebrew, איכה), the contrast between former glory and present circumstance, a description of misery, and the gloating onlookers. One of the only breaks with the genre is to blame

Zion for her present state, which would have no place in a pure dirge.
The scene is dismal, and what biblical scholars call the qinah (dirgelike) meter of the poetry is entirely appropriate for the tone of desolation. Yet there is already a certain amount of ambiguity with
regard to genre even in the opening verses. For as much as the funeral dirge can be discerned here, the primary element that grounds
all dirges is missing: a death. The ostensible event that necessitates a
dirge is the death of an individual or personified individual, or, as in
the derivative oracles against the nations, the ironically anticipated
death. But even before the chapter switches voices and genres into
lament in verses 12–22, one is aware that Zion has in fact survived.
Given the deathly scene surveyed by the poet, the formal and thematic characteristics of the dirge do not seem entirely out of place;
nevertheless, the dirge, which should properly signal the death of
Zion, takes place while she is yet alive.

While Zion survives in the dirge of the poet, the import of this really becomes apparent only in the second half of chapter 1. It is here
that Zion emerges most forcefully as a speaking subject, and it is here
that elements of the funeral song increasingly give way to the elements of lament. The scene of death implied by the dirge, already
undercut by the presence of Zion, begins to open out toward life
even more. Not only is the one who should be dead alive, but she is
speaking, and speaking vigorously. The genre of lament, like the
dirge, arises out of pain and knows much about death. Yet unlike the
dirge, its primary aim is life. The lament addresses God and expects
an answer. Westermann writes:

> There is not a single Psalm of Lament that stops with lamentation.
> Lamentation has no meaning in and of itself. That it functions as an ap-
> peal is evident in its structure. What the lament is concerned with is not
> a description of one's own sufferings or with self-pity, but with the
> removal of the suffering itself.[13]

While Westermann likely overstates the case, particularly with regard to the book of Lamentations, the basic point that the lament as
a genre looks beyond the situation of death is important. The dirge
of the poet recedes as the primary mode of discourse in the face of
Zion's survival.

Zion's direct address to the Lord, which form-critically belongs in the realm of the lament, has already infiltrated the dirge of the poet as early as verse 9. The verse begins with a two-line summary of how Zion has so far been presented: her state of uncleanness is reiterated; she is blamed for this uncleanness ("she did not think of her future"); the reversal of fortunes is restated ("she has come down astonishingly"); and she is once more said to have "none to comfort her." But there is a radical shift in verse 9c when what is unmistakably the voice of Zion herself interrupts the poet. This interruption is short, only two cola, but nonetheless compelling:

> See, O LORD, my suffering—
> how the enemy triumphs.

The poet's monopoly on the reader is momentarily broken; the one spoken about now becomes the one who speaks. Likewise, while the poet has spoken *about* YHWH in the dirge, it Zion who first speaks *to* YHWH in the form of a lament.[14]

Though the intrusion of Zion in verse 1:9 is brief, it may be taken as setting in motion the transition from dirge to lament, from death to life, that Lamentations 1 and 2 will develop further. For example, while the poem seems to resume the dirge in verse 10, there is a slight indication that the persona of the poet, if not that of YHWH, has also become concerned with the outward movement of the lament in contrast to the dirge. For in verse 10 the poet uncharacteristically speaks to YHWH, using the second-person form of address for the first time.

> She has seen nations come into
> her holy place—
> about whom you commanded,
> they shall not come into your assembly.

Up to this point the persona of the poet has employed third-person verbs only, with Zion breaking the pattern by addressing YHWH directly. On the heels of Zion's speech comes the poet's own direct speech to YHWH, indicating a beginning of a conformity of language between the two personae that will become more pronounced in later verses.

The poet's growing concern for life as well as his awareness of the threat of death both are present in verse 11 as well. He describes the inhabitants of Zion as having kept themselves alive, but only at great cost. The climax of the poet's speech is in 11b:

> They have given their precious things for food,
>   in order to keep themselves alive.

The connotation of the Hebrew word used here for "precious things" (מחמדיהם) is debatable. It may mean expensive or treasured possessions, as it does in 1 Kings 20:6 and Joel 4:5, or it may mean children, as it does in Hosea 9:16. One need not decide between these two connotations, as the poetry is able to carry both simultaneously. Indeed, the two meanings are clearly juxtaposed in Hosea 9, where verse 16 refers to offspring but verse 6 refers to objects of silver. Given the poetic strategy of personification, both connotations are likely on the horizon of the poetry in Lamentations 1 as well. The connotation of "treasures" is aligned with the destruction of an actual city, while the connotation of "children" is aligned with the city in its personification as a woman. The second connotation makes the line bitterly ironic: only by sacrificing a future survival can the semblance of a present survival be maintained. Moreover, the trace of children in the phrase "precious things" anticipates 2:20 and 4:10, where children themselves are said to be eaten by their mothers.[15]

The second intrusion by the figure of Zion, in 1:11c, manifests an even stronger move away from the dirge and into the lament, the form of which dominates the remainder of the chapter. Zion's initial address to YHWH in verse 9c, with its single imperative to "see" her pain, is echoed and compounded in the address in verse 11c, with its double imperative for YHWH to "see" (ראה) and "pay attention to" (והביטה) how abject Zion has become. As with the second-person address of YHWH, the accusation against God that follows in verses 12–16 is a characteristic element of the lament genre, containing the typical threefold concern for the agony of the one suffering, the relationship of God to the suffering, and the mention of enemies.[16]

The voice of Zion holds sway for most of the second half of Lamentations 1, effectively excluding the elements of the dirge, based as they are in the finality of death. The traditional "setting in life" (Sitz im Leben) of a dirge is the funeral, where it serves as a stage in the work of mourning, a stage that one passes through in order to "overcome" the loss of the individual. In psychoanalytic terms, the ego attempts to break off its overwhelming attachment to the one lost.[17] But as we have seen, Zion is not yet lost, and her move to direct lament in verses 12–16 forestalls the premature mourning that might allow either the poet or the reader to overcome her death.[18]

Although the poet interjects in verse 17, mirroring Zion's intrusion (in verse 9c) into his speech in the first half of the chapter, with possible allusions to death,[19] such allusions are passed over as Zion speaks once more in verse 18. Any question of a genuine dirge over the death of Zion is here put to rest, though in keeping with the poem's awareness of the infiltration of death into the realm of life, Zion laments:

> Outside, the sword slays—
> indoors, death.[20] (1:20c)

Death has crossed the final border and entered even the safe haven of the house.

The final section of chapter 1 represents well the outward reach of the genre of lament. Zion employs the standard elements of a lament: a summons to participation (18b), a plea for YHWH to take notice (20a), and a petition for reprisal against the enemy (22a).[21] This final section of chapter 1 also represents well the manner in which the genre of lament intersects with the literature of survival. From the portrayal of a world hostile to life, to the attempt to sway its audience, to the undeniable dream of revenge, Zion's voice is that of the survivor. Holocaust survivor Jorge Semprun echoes Zion's appeal for revenge: "There's no point trying to understand the SS. It is enough just to exterminate them."[22] Jean Améry, though admitting that "resentment blocks the exit to the genuine human dimension, the future" and is therefore not something to be nurtured or desired by survivors, nonetheless goes on to speak of his "conviction that loudly proclaimed readiness for reconciliation by Nazi victims can only be either insanity and indifference to life or the masochistic conversion of a suppressed *genuine* demand for revenge."[23] I considered the commingling of life and death and the desire to persuade in the previous chapter on survival, but it must be noted that Zion's call for revenge also has its place in the literature of survival.

In keeping with the movement away from the dirge (with its

world of death) and toward the lament (with its drive for life),
Lamentations 2 continues the mixture of forms, or genres, but does
so with the emphasis on lament. Indeed, as Westermann has noted,
"In broad outline, the structure of Lamentations 2 corresponds to
that of the communal lament. Only the mournful cry at the beginning really belongs to the dirge."[24] The presence of "Alas" (איכה) at
the start of chapter 2 functions as a parallel to the start of chapter 1
as well as establishing the relationship with the dirge. Also preserved
from the dirge, in verses 1–8 particularly, is the contrast between former and present status. God has thrown down the "splendor of Israel" from heaven to earth (2:1). God has torn down the strongholds
of Judah. No longer an ally, "God has become an enemy" (2:5). The
reversal is made most explicit and most far-reaching in verse 7:

> The Lord has rejected his altar,
> > spurned his sanctuary.
> He has given the walls of her citadels
> > into the hand of the enemy.
> They shout in the house of the LORD,
> > as though it were a feast day.

All that was formerly honored and held sacred is now rejected and
profaned. The extent to which the city's fortunes have been reversed
is epitomized by the portrayal of the temple, which should be the
site of celebration, as the site of desecration.

In spite of these elements of the dirge in Lamentations 2, it is clear
that the form of lament becomes more prominent. For example, the
entire section of 2:1–10 represents an accusation against God, found
in most laments, that has been transformed into a third-person description of misery. Though retaining elements from his dirgelike
speech from Lamentations 1, the poet in chapter 2 begins to take
into account the fact that the city still exists—that Zion remains
alive—in spite of its dismal state. Language of elegy is progressively
transformed into the language of lament, coming to a culmination
in the second half of the chapter (which I will treat more thoroughly
in the third section of this chapter).

Although it may well be that chapters 1 and 2 were written as separate compositions, as they stand now they manifest together a similar
mixture of the forms of lament and dirge, with an emphasis on the

movement from dirge to lament. Thus, when read together these two chapters draw the reader into the world of survival literature, a world characterized by death in the midst of life and life in the midst of death.[25]

The Presentation of Pain in Lamentations 1 and 2

As literature of survival, chapters 1 and 2 of Lamentations not only demonstrate a commingling of life and death, but they also demonstrate the strong desire, found throughout survival literature, to make present to the reader the pain and suffering of survivors. In order to understand Lamentations 1 and 2 properly, one must maintain the distinction between the "presentation" of pain and the "interpretation" of pain. Both the presentation of pain and the interpretation of pain exist in Lamentations 1 and 2, but the extent and significance of each have been given very uneven treatment in modern critical interpretation. Biblical scholars have tended to focus on the *interpretation* of pain, and not surprisingly they have done so primarily by explaining pain and suffering as resulting from the guilt of the sufferer. Taking a clue from the literature of survival, however, I will refocus interpretation of chapters 1 and 2 around the *presentation* of pain, thereby balancing the penchant of biblical scholars to seek explanation for suffering and instead offering a fuller and more nuanced reading of these chapters.

Terrence Des Pres's evaluation of the role played by pain in the literature of survival offers a sobering corrective to the view that suffering can, or even must, be absorbed into a system of meaning (whether theological or otherwise). Des Pres writes:

> One of the strongest themes in the literature of survival is that pain is senseless; that a suffering so vast is completely without value as *suffering*. The survivor, then, is a disturber of the peace.[26]

Such an evaluation is very different from how pain and suffering are treated by biblical scholars, who seem overeager to make the move from the fact of pain to the recognition of guilt and subsequently to repentance. I contend that viewing Lamentations 1 and 2 from the perspective of the literature of survival enables one to perceive aspects of the presentation of suffering in Lamentations that have been obscured by the theological presuppositions of biblical scholars.

The survivor's desire to witness to pain rather than to find mean-

ing in it can be seen clearly in the speeches of Zion in chapters 1
and 2. Especially striking in this regard are the two initial interruptive statements by which personified Zion enters the poetry as a
speaking subject.

> See, O LORD, my suffering—
>> how the enemy triumphs. (1:9c)
> See, O LORD, and pay attention—
>> how abject I have become. (1:12c)

In the previous section of this chapter, I identified these imperatives
to YHWH as the beginning of a strong move away from the death represented by the genre of the funeral song and toward the drive for
life represented by the genre of lament. The move, however, is not
easy or automatic, but proceeds through the survivor's acute experience of suffering. Such suffering must be "seen," in the words of
Zion. The lament requires that the experience of the one lamenting
be looked at and acknowledged.

The importance of this requirement that suffering and pain be acknowledged is demonstrated by the compounding of imperatives in
the beginning of Zion's first speech in Lamentations 1. The single
imperative in 1:9c for YHWH to "see" (ראה) becomes the double imperative in 1:11c for YHWH to "see and pay attention" (והביטה ראה).
This double imperative is then immediately repeated (in an inverted
form) to the passersby in 1:12:

> Pay attention and see![27]
> Is there any pain like my pain,
>> like my continual suffering?
> Which the LORD inflicted on me,
>> on the day of his wrath? (1:12)

The five imperatives in a row, combined with the double repetition
of "pain" and the use of the harsh words "suffering" and "inflicted,"
lend a rhetorical significance to Zion's presentation of pain *as pain*,
rather than as the raw material for ruminations on guilt. As long as
the voice of the poet holds the reader's attention in the opening
verses of chapter 1, the pain of Zion has been kept at arm's length.
Not only is her suffering described in the third person, but the poet
is wont to make sense of Zion's suffering with reference to her sins

(1:8), rebelliousness (1:5), or impurity (1:9). The irruption of first-person misery into the poem via the voice of Zion, however, defers all such sense making. Zion is, to use Des Pres's phrase, a "disturber of the peace" in that she will not let the subject of her suffering be settled so easily. Unlike the poet in verses 1:1–11, Zion makes little correlation between her sins and her suffering. Zion's first speech in 1:12–16, outside of one textually very uncertain phrase in 1:14,[28] contains no reference to sin whatsoever. In other words, there is no attempt here to interpret or explain suffering.

Instead of explanations for suffering, one finds in Zion's speech an accusation against God combined with a terrifying description of misery. The command to "see" gives way in 1:13–15 to the description of what may be seen, as the character of Zion gives concrete detail to fill out her general statement in verse 12 that YHWH has afflicted her. While the poet tended to focus in verses 1–11 on the human agents of destruction—referring repeatedly to foes, enemies, betrayers, despisers, invaders in the temple, and exile among the nations, but only once naming YHWH as the subject of affliction—Zion repeatedly names YHWH as the one who afflicts and she repeatedly attributes active verbs of violence to YHWH.

In this section one begins to feel more keenly the import of the author's use of the poetic technique of personification to convey the destruction of a city, as the language of actual physical pain that can be experienced only by living beings pervades the accusation against God. Thus, in 1:13 Zion portrays herself as being attacked by YHWH-as-warrior, who catches her feet in a net and hurls her backward. Fire, no doubt a vivid image in reference to the destruction of cities, is said in this verse to penetrate to the very bones of Zion. At the same time as the personification allows for the presentation of the pain of the city itself, it also allows one to continue to speak of the suffering of the inhabitants of the city, who are portrayed as the children of personified Zion (בחורי, 1:15; בני, 1:16). The first speech of Zion presents to the reader the sheer fact of pain, told from the perspective of a figure who has survived that pain. It leads to a climax in verse 16:

> For these things I weep . . . My eyes, my eyes!
>> They stream with tears.
> How far from me is one to comfort,
>> one to restore my life.

> My children are ravaged,[29]
>   the enemy has triumphed.

The twofold cry, "my eyes, my eyes" (עיני עיני), is by no means
simply a "clear case of dittography,"[30] but is another way of intensifying the presentation of pain and grief.[31] Zion's lament is that of
a survivor—one who has lived through death and destruction—
culminating with a mother's wailing over the loss of her children.

It is important to note that the character of Zion, for all her challenging of YHWH, never claims complete innocence. Zion's lament
in 1:18–22, following the brief interruption of the poet in 1:17 (to
be treated more fully below), begins by acknowledging that "YHWH
is in the right" and that she has been "rebellious." And at the end of
her speech in 1:22 she admits that YHWH afflicted her because of her
rebelliousness; though it must be noted that the admission is in the
context of a call for a similar affliction on her enemies. Zion is, of
course, not a completely autonomous figure divorced from the culture of lament characteristic of the ancient Near East in which the
book of Lamentations was written. Zion is rather a literary persona
created by an author who participated in that common culture,
which included the notion of divine punishment on the basis of human misbehavior or disloyalty. While participating in these cultural
and theological presuppositions, the author nevertheless saw fit to
shift the focus of these poems away from the issue of guilt and toward the experience of pain and suffering, regardless of guilt. Even,
for example, in 1:18–22 where the figure of Zion refers to sin and
rebelliousness, the rhetoric continues to shift to the experience and
extent of pain. Immediately on the heels of the admission of YHWH's
"righteousness" (or perhaps "victory") in 1:18a come echoes of her
earlier imperatives to the passersby:

> Listen, each and every one,
>   look at my agony.
> My young women and my young men alike
>   have gone into captivity.

Also repeated from her earlier description of pain is the desertion
of allies and the hunger of the city's inhabitants (1:19). The
imperative for YHWH to see her distress is repeated in verse 20
(ראה יהוה כי־צר־לי), as is the leitmotif "there was no one to com-

fort me" in verse 21 (אין מנחם לי). Brief allusions to guilt in Zion's second speech thus give way to extended expressions of misery and desolation.

I do not mean to claim that the notion of guilt in the book of Lamentations or the ancient Near Eastern genre of lament is the same as that in twentieth-century literature of survival. I admit the very real differences between the two, even as I suggest that one might nevertheless learn something about Lamentations by reading it alongside twentieth-century survival literature. A brief comparison is thus in order. Des Pres writes:

> With very few exceptions, the testimony of survivors does not concern itself with guilt of any sort. Their books neither admonish nor condemn nor beg forgiveness; not because survivors are drained of their humanity, but because their attention lies wholly elsewhere.[32]

Compare this with the judgment of Westermann concerning Zion's admission of sin in verse 18.

> Just how important the acknowledgment of guilt is for Lam 1 has already been shown (with ref. to vv 5 and 9). Here, at the high point of the whole song, this motif is brought into conjunction with an acknowledgment of the justice of God's ways such that the whole preceding lament is set off: God must act in this way, because we have transgressed against his word.[33]

Des Pres is arguing against the prevalent concept of "survivor guilt," the notion that those who have lived through atrocities such as mass murder are plagued by a sense of guilt over the fact that while so many others died, they somehow escaped alive. Des Pres does not claim that such guilt is nonexistent, but rather that it is not the primary drive of survivor testimony, which is chiefly devoted to conveying the experience of atrocity and survival. What Des Pres is arguing *against* in the reading of twentieth-century survival literature—the elevating of the single theme of guilt to the status of an interpretive key—is precisely what Westermann is *demonstrating* in his readings of the biblical laments. Westermann has taken the element of guilt, which is undeniably present, and made it the lens through which all else is read. This element becomes the "high point" of the chapter and sets off "the whole preceding lament."

Both Des Pres and Westermann likely overstate their cases. In the current debate over the nature and extent of survivor guilt, Des Pres's statement would no doubt need to be nuanced. As a biblical scholar, however, I find that it offers a helpful corrective to the statement of Westermann. The persona of Zion does indeed admit her sins or disobedience. Such an admission is a genre convention of the lament, and Lamentations 1 and 2 does not excise it. Yet rather than making her sins the primary concern of her speeches, she admits them flatly and not altogether wholeheartedly. Westermann's celebration of guilt as the hermeneutical key to the entire chapter is unwarranted. Using Des Pres's analysis to nuance Westermann's, it is clear that Zion, as a survivor, does not "beg forgiveness." And as I will argue below, it also becomes clear that Zion's attention, and that of the poet, ultimately lies wholly elsewhere.

The insistence on the sheer fact of suffering, with little reference to its deservedness or merits, becomes even more apparent in chapter 2 of Lamentations. On the heels of Zion's utterances, which are densely packed with the presentation of pain, the poet's language changes significantly, leaving behind the interpretation of suffering in terms of guilt and placing the focus on the presentation of divine wrath and Zion's pain. In a stance similar to that of Zion, who in chapter 1 emphatically identified Yhwh as the source of destruction, the poet now portrays God as an enemy warrior in line after line. Verses 1–4, for example, are a poetic whirlwind of fire and wrath. Verse 1: Yhwh "in his wrath" (באפו) has shamed Zion, and has forgotten his footstool "on the day of his wrath" (ביום אפו). Verse 2: "In his fury" (בעברתו) Yhwh has razed Judah's defenses. Verse 3: Yhwh has cut down "in blazing wrath" (בחרי-אף) the horn of Israel, and has "burned (ויבער) against Israel like a blazing fire (כאש להבה), consuming on all sides." Verse 4: Yhwh pours out against Zion "his wrath like fire (כאש חמתו)." The English language is exhausted in an attempt to describe the destructive inferno unleashed by the Lord's anger.

With its double use of "swallowed up" (בלע), verse 5 serves as an introduction to the systematic dismantling of the city that follows. First, Yhwh eradicates the public institutions in verses 6–7, eliminating all public modes of access to the divine: Yhwh's "booth" and "(tent of) meeting" are destroyed, festivals and Sabbaths are ended, the altar and sanctuary are rejected, and the temple desecrated. Sec-

ond, YHWH demolishes the actual physical structures of the city in
verses 8–9a: walls and ramparts languish, gates are sunk into the
ground with their bars smashed to bits. Third, the conquered state
of the inhabitants of the city is described in their abandonment by
YHWH in verses 9b–10: the king and the princes are exiled, the
teachers of Torah are no more, the prophets receive no vision, the
elders sit about in mourning, and the young women lower their
heads to the ground. So while the opening speeches by the poet in
both chapters 1 and 2 are similar in their description of misery, destruction, and death, there is a noticeable change in the poet's voice.
Not only does the poet attribute the destruction to YHWH in chapter
2, but any reference to the sin of Zion drops away. This change in the
persona of the poet, as he begins to conform more and more to the
speech of Zion, leads into the next element of the literature of survival that is manifested in Lamentations: the desire to persuade.

The Rhetoric of Persuasion and the Children of Zion

The description of pain in literature of survival exists, in the first instance, for its own sake. That is, such description needs no other val-
idation than the fact and experience of the pain that has given rise to
it. But in many cases, as I described above in chapter 1, literature of
survival functions not only to describe but to persuade; the literature
moves from the basic need to give voice to pain to the project of giving testimony or bearing witness. In this second function, description may serve an end beyond itself: that of drawing the reader, to
the extent that it is possible to do so, into the experience of survival
and to make the concerns of the survivor the concerns of the reader
as well. Des Pres, once again, states this well:

> In the literature of survival we find an image of things so grim, so heart-
> breaking, so starkly unbearable, that inevitably the survivor's scream be-
> gins to be our own. When this happens the role of the spectator is no
> longer enough.[34]

This desire to persuade is one of the most striking correspondences
between Lamentations 1 and 2 and modern literature of survival,
though the differences also must be kept in mind.

One significant difference between the book of Lamentations and
modern literature of survival, in their respective tasks of persuasion,

is the issue of whom they are trying to persuade. Insofar as modern literature of survival has a persuasive function, it is addressed to those who did not share the experience of suffering that it describes and who are not, for the most part, to be considered survivors. By contrast Lamentations, though also likely written by survivors of the destruction it describes, is written (at least originally) for other survivors as well. The status of Lamentations as liturgical poetry gives it a different initial rhetorical situation from modern literature of survival. The one whom these poems, as liturgical laments, are desperately trying to persuade is God.[35] It is my argument that the task of persuasion is compounded in Lamentations 1 and 2 to an exceptional degree, both in the internal workings of the poetry and in their afterlife. One finds not only an appeal to YHWH to see and to intervene to alleviate the suffering described but, failing that, the task of persuasion implicates in a remarkably self-referential way the persona of the poet. And as the history of interpretation shows, Lamentations does indeed get bound up with the persuasion of readers who did not share the original experience, whether or not such persuasion was on the horizon of its initial rhetorical situation. I argue as well that the survival of Zion's children occupies a privileged and critical role in this rhetoric of persuasion, representing a key to the literary and emotional structure of Lamentations 1 and 2. As the drive for life becomes more apparent in the shift in genre from the dirge to the lament and in the increasing emphasis on the function of persuasion, the drive for life also becomes more apparent in the content of Zion's lament. The laments of both Zion and the poet culminate in a concern for the lives of the children who are dying in the streets.

The subject of Zion's children is first raised in the poet's opening speech in chapter 1, where the fact that "infants have gone into captivity" (עולליה הלכו שבי; 1:5) is presented as part of the third-person description of the destruction. Here it seems to hold no special place in the description. Zion's first extended speech in 1:12–16, however, comes to a rhetorical, and one could say an emotional, climax in her emphasis on the fate of her children. I refer to verse 16 (cited and translated above) as the rhetorical climax of her speech because it occurs there as the culmination of her accusation against God and is marked for emphasis as the point at which the poet breaks

into her speech. I allude to the emotional aspect of the verse because
it is here that Zion describes a sort of upheaval of passion: "For these
things I weep . . . My eyes, my eyes! They stream with tears." Given
the lament's function of persuasion, the interruption of the poet
coming just at this climactic point of the chapter is no accident. Zion
has appealed to YHWH twice (1:9 and 1:11), but the reader is given
no indication of a response or a shift toward praise or a vow of confidence that might indicate a salvation oracle, that is, a sign that
YHWH has heard or intends to answer Zion.

Instead of some indication of the desired response from YHWH,
the reader meets in 1:17 the persona of the poet once again, thereby
beginning the inscription of the rhetoric of persuasion but with the
poet standing in for YHWH as the one who is persuaded. The poet's
language in verse 17 has begun to reflect, albeit subtly, the presence
of the Zion persona in the poem. For example, in addition to the leitmotif of "none to comfort," the poet repeats in verse 17 language
that had previously clustered around the initial intrusion of Zion into
the poem in 1:9c. While the enemy spread (פרש) his hands over
Zion's precious things in verse 10, it is now Zion who desperately
spreads out (פרשה) her hands, perhaps in a futile attempt to protect
herself or to find something that might keep her from falling. And
while in verse 10 the invading army is presented as those whom
YHWH has commanded (צוה) to not come in, in verse 17 the poet
speaks of YHWH commanding (צוה) the enemy to surround Jacob.
The persona of the poet has, of course, already been recruited to the
task of witnessing to the destruction via his role as the speaker of the
dirge in 1:1–11. Though making reference to the sin and guilt of
the city, he nevertheless expresses genuine grief at the reversal of fate
that Zion has experienced. As the genre of the poetry moves from
dirge toward lament, the poet moves also from one who elegizes
Zion to one who laments in solidarity with her and even attempts,
albeit futilely, to provide the response to the lament that Zion is seeking. Using Des Pres's language, while it is wrong to say that the poet
has been up until this point a "spectator," it is true that as Zion's situation becomes "starkly unbearable" her scream begins to be the
poet's scream as well. Only a hint of such a persuasion exists at this
point, but it is a hint that gets fully developed in the larger movement
of chapters 1 and 2. For example, although the poet's voice is given

the most space in chapter 2, his speech becomes progressively more like the speech of Zion in chapter 1. As Westermann notes, the poet's description of misery in the first half of Lamentations 2, especially in its repeated portrayal of what "Y HWH has done," corresponds closely to an accusation of God. Thus, the form of the poet's speech here has begun to resemble the form of the speech of Zion in chapter 1.

The intensification of personal, emotional speech on the part of the poet—in other words, his alignment with the experience of Zion—comes to a head in verses 11–12. Like the first chapter, this halfway point in the poem marks a climax and transition. In the face of the plight of Zion, the voice of the poet here expresses precisely the sort of emotional upheaval that we saw with the persona of Zion herself in 1:16.

> My eyes are spent with tears,
>> my stomach churns,
> my bile is poured out on the ground,
>> because of the brokenness of the daughter
>> of my people,
> broken over the children and the infants
>> collapsing in the streets of the city.
> They kept saying to their mothers,
>> "Where is bread and wine?"
> as they collapsed like the wounded
>> in the squares of the city,
> as their lives ran out
>> in the bosoms of their mothers. (2:11–12)

That the poet has been forcefully recruited to the plight of Zion is indicated by the way that his words, at this important juncture, echo closely the earlier words of Zion. Even as Zion's eyes flowed with tears (1:16), so the poet's eyes are spent with tears. The poet also employs the same phrase used by Zion in 1:20, "my stomach churns" (חמרמרו מעי), to describe his physical or emotional distress. The scream of Zion has, almost literally, become the scream of the poet. But most significantly, what magnifies the emotional register both for Zion in 1:16 and the poet in 2:11–12 is the image of children under threat. It may be that the passage under consideration not only portrays the poet's emotional state as similar to Zion's, but explicitly calls attention to the function of persuasion. Notice that the Hebrew particle עַל ("because of") in verse 11 introduces the causative clause that follows: it is because of the brokenness of Zion, here called the "daughter of my people," that the persona of the poet is in such distress. What follows this line may well be another causative clause, introduced by the infinitive construct of the Hebrew term עטף with a bet prefix ("collapsing"), which may be taken as a reference back to the cause of Zion's distress. On this reading, reflected in my translation above, a causal chain exists in the verse, in which the cause of the poet's distress is identified as the brokenness of Zion, and the cause of the brokenness of Zion is identified as the children collapsing like the wounded in the squares of the city. Thus it is Zion's presentation of the plight of her children that has recruited the poet so forcefully. Since the lament as a genre is concerned to get a response from God to the suffering it describes, the poet is modeling the response to Zion's lament that should come from God.

In a now-classic article on the theological implications of the Holocaust, Irving Greenberg has suggested the following as a working principle: "No statement, theological or otherwise, should be made that would not be credible in the presence of the burning children."[36] The force of Greenberg's criterion, of course, is to point up that no speech is adequate as an explanation of such suffering. Immediately following the emotional climax of 2:11–12, the poet of Lamentations comes to a similar conclusion in verse 13.

> What can I say for you, to what can
>   I compare you, daughter Jerusalem?
> To what can I liken you,
>   that I may comfort you, Daughter Zion?
> For your breach is as vast as the sea—
>   who could heal you? (2:13)

For the first time in the book the poet acknowledges his own subjectivity. He speaks in the first person and refers in fact to his task *as poet*: to attempt to translate into language the suffering he sees. Also for the first time the poet makes explicit his dialogical relationship to the figure of Zion by addressing her in the second person. So the task of the poet is not only to search for language adequate to the destruction, but to do so in order to console Zion. Against his earlier statements that there was none to comfort her, the poet here explic-

itly attempts to fill the role of "comforter" (ואנחמך; 2:13b). With
acute poignancy, however, the poet admits at the same time the fu-
tility of his attempts at consolation. The questions of verse 13 are
rhetorical: only the inadequate can be said; only the inadequate
comparison can be made; there is no healing for a breach as vast as
the sea. The poet is caught in the survivor's dilemma. "But how is
one to say, how is one to communicate that which by its very nature
defies language? How is one to tell without betraying the dead, without betraying oneself?"[37] To speak is to betray the memory of the
dead, for all metaphors are wanting. To remain silent, however, is a
worse betrayal: "[h]ence the vital necessity to bear witness."[38]

One can hardly consider the poet's predicament in relation to
twentieth-century survival literature without thinking of Theodor
Adorno's famous remark from 1949 that to write poetry after
Auschwitz is barbaric.[39] After much literal-minded criticism of the
remark, Adorno wrote the following in 1966:

> Perennial suffering has as much right to expression as a tortured man has
> to scream; hence it may have been wrong to say that after Auschwitz you
> could no longer write poems. But it is not wrong to raise the less cultural
> question whether after Auschwitz you can go on living.[40]

So the poet continues, as even Adorno conceded must be done.
His continued speech in 2:14–17 surveys the cast of characters and
further elaborates Zion's destitute condition: the prophets are
found wanting, as they prophesied only "emptiness and whitewash"
(2:14); the passersby only clap and mock Jerusalem, reveling in her
downfall (2:15); and the enemies, of course, jeer and gloat over
their triumph (2:16). The poet comes finally in verse 17 to YHWH,
but the only one who might be able to comfort Zion is also the author of the wreckage and the drive behind the enemies' victory:
"The LORD has done what he planned . . . he has torn down without
pity . . . he has made your enemies gloat over you" (2:17).

Having taken up the cause of Zion, but able neither to find a comforter nor to comfort Zion adequately himself, the poet urges Zion,
with a final intensification of rhetoric at the end of his speech, to cry
out herself once more to YHWH (2:18–19).

> Cry out to the LORD from the heart,[41]
>   wall of Daughter Zion.

Shed tears like a torrent,
    day and night!
Give yourself no rest,
    no relief for your eyes.
Rise up! Wail in the night,
    at the start of every watch.
Pour out your heart like water
    before the LORD.
Lift your hands to him
    for the lives of your infants,
who collapse from hunger
    at the corner of every street.

The poet has just exhausted the Hebrew language in an attempt to find enough metaphors to depict YHWH the arch-warrior; yet it is this same YHWH to whom Zion is to appeal.

This sort of appeal to the destroyer to become the one to heal is a conventional element in ancient Near Eastern laments. But can one see here what Westermann repeatedly calls a plea for "God's gracious intervention"?[42] That is surely too benign a characterization. The notion of an abused and violated woman turning for help to her abuser, and the one who abused her children, should inspire in the modern reader something less than the notion of gracious intervention. Westermann is, even more than most biblical scholars, heavily invested in the form-critical judgment that lament is a stage through which the prayer moves on the way back to a restored relationship with God.[43] Essential to Westermann's analysis of the structure of laments is the transition to a vow of praise (in the communal laments) or to praise itself (in the individual laments).[44] In fact, Westermann identifies 2:18–19 explicitly with the move to praise found in psalmic laments: "Form-critically speaking, these lines correspond to the imperatively-worded summons to praise known from the Psalms."[45] Even Westermann, however, must admit that what we find in these verses, and in Zion's response in 2:20–22, is far from praise. So he judges that, "in terms of their content, these imperatives more closely resemble the call to wait patiently upon Yahweh."[46] But certainly this final section of chapter 2 no more advocates a patient waiting than it does a stance of praise toward YHWH.

At this point, the project of reading for survival in Lamentations

can be instructive once again. It is significant that there is no mention
here of "comfort." It is not inconceivable, as I note above, that in the
context of ancient Near Eastern laments the destroyer could also be
imagined as the potential comforter (see also for example Isa.
54:7–8). In Lamentations 3 one can identify a similar dynamic. In
Lamentations 1 and 2, however, that is not what happens. Indeed,
2:13 tells the reader nothing if not that the very category of comfort
has been called into question. Neither is there any indication in the
poet's urging (or in Zion's response in 2:20–22) that a move to praise
is on the horizon. No, the rhetorical move imagined by the poet is for
Zion to affront YHWH with the intolerable suffering of children, precisely *on behalf of the children* (על נפש עולליך). As the chapter moves toward its close, what has become clearly at stake is neither a reconciled
relationship with YHWH nor the possibility of praise, but the very survival of the children who are dying in the street.

What makes the image of suffering children so important for the
literary and emotional structure of Lamentations 1 and 2 is the way
it works on both a literal and a figurative level. Children are, of
course, among the literal victims of the destruction of a city and represent perhaps the most poignant image of such victims even in our
time. The force of the image is compounded, however, by the poetic
mode of personifying the city as a grieving mother. The children,
while retaining the concrete and disturbing images associated with
the destruction, also become "summary" figures for the totality of
the city's losses. The privileged image of a mother's loss of children
serves to express how devastating it is for a city to lose not only altar
and sanctuary, but prophet, priest, and king, in addition to the citizens, young and old, of the city.

The subtle artistry of the poetry's emphasis on the image of children nicely sets off its more forceful rhetoric of 2:18–19. Thus for
example the occurrence of the *Leitwort* "pour out" (Hebrew root:
שפך) at this critical point in the poem represents a nexus of interre-
lations between the characters. Indeed, it is possible to see each character defined by what he or she is said to pour out. Mother Zion is
told to "pour out (שפך) your heart like water . . . for the lives (נפש)
of your children." In 2:12 it is precisely the "lives (נפש) of the children" that are being "poured out (שפך) in the bosoms of their
mothers." Moreover, in that same passage it is the pouring out of the

children's lives that moves the poet to "pour out" (שפך) his grief
(2:11). In sharp contrast, when the word שפך is used with YHWH as
the subject, it describes the pouring out of YHWH's raging fire (2:4).
This is a far cry from Westermann's "call to wait patiently upon Yahweh." There is no pretension of reconciliation or praise here, but a
central concern for the lives of the children. It is the threat to the
children that led to Zion's breaking down into tears in 1:16, as well
as the poet's brief interruption into Zion's speech in 1:17 where he
first names YHWH as the purveyor of destruction. It is also the perishing children that lead to the poet's own breakdown in 2:11. Perhaps, then, the lives of the children will be enough to move even
YHWH.

Chapter 2 closes with Zion responding to the poet's urging, culminating in the most accusatory passage in the book.

> Look, O LORD, and pay attention to whom it is
> that you have so ruthlessly afflicted!
> Alas! Women are eating their offspring,
> the children they have borne. (2:20a–b)

Zion employs the same imperative that she did in 1:11c in an attempt to command the attention of YHWH and to gain the survival of
her children. Translators have typically watered down the accusatory
nature of the first line by rendering the second colon as "to whom
you have done this" (JPSV; NRSV). But the Hebrew verb that is used
here (עלל) carries the much stronger force of "to afflict" or "to
abuse" and may even imply capriciousness.[47] In Judges 19:25, for
example, the same verb is used to describe the fate of the Levite's
concubine, where it is a parallel to the verb "rape." In 1 Samuel 31:4
it is used by Saul to describe what he imagines the Philistines will do
to him if he is caught, and it is here used in parallel to "run through"
with a sword. In Job 16:15 it is used in the midst of a passage that
describes God's rushing Job like a warrior, piercing his kidneys and
showing no mercy, despite Job's protestations of innocence. The
verb עללת (pronounced 'ôlaltā) is sardonically placed in Lamentations 2:20a in a parallel position with the similarly written and
sounding noun עללי (pronounced 'ōlalê, "children," 2:20b), thereby
contrasting the ruthlessness of YHWH with the suffering of children,
and making clear that these are the ones whom YHWH is afflicting.

Zion continues in the final section to elaborate on the suffering of the population: priest and prophet are slain in the sanctuary, old and young alike die in the streets, young women and young men are fallen by the sword. The function of children as summary figures, or symbolic condensations, of the entire population of the city is indicated by the bracketing of "priest and prophet" (2:20c) and "young and old" (2:21a) by the images of perishing children in 2:20a and 2:22c. This privileged image of loss surrounds the others, not in order to exceed them but rather to gather up and express the multiform dimensions of grief and loss to which the destruction of the city has given rise.

In the final lines of her speech, the persona of Zion employs ironically the language of the cult: after slaughtering her inhabitants, YHWH invited people from all around, "as if on a feast-day" (כיום מועד; 2:22a). A feast does indeed take place, but it is a gruesome perversion of the cult that affronts the reader in the last line of verse 22: "those whom I bore and reared, the enemy has consumed!" Zion's final speech of 2:20–22, bounded at beginning and end by the cannibalizing of children, is the last we hear from her in the book of Lamentations. Her penultimate line (2:22b) rings fitting as a summary of Lamentations 1 and 2: "none survived or escaped."

From Literature of Survival to the Survival of Literature

From the opening as a dirge, to the final, gripping lament of Zion, the first two chapters of Lamentations demonstrate in progressively stronger terms their status as literature of survival. As the elements of the dirge fall away in chapter 2, the drive for survival moves from the abstract to the concrete, culminating in the faces of the children of Zion. In this movement the poems also model the way in which the survivor attempts to recruit the detached observer, for there can be no doubt that Zion's scream, to use Des Pres's language, becomes the scream of the poet. Yet despite this increasingly stronger movement toward life, and despite the alignment of the poet with the experience of Zion and her lament for the lives of her children, the drive for survival is frustrated and the final verdict is one of death. Both Zion and the poet seem to have failed to affect the one who counts most, the one who is thought able to remove the suffering and save the children: God.

The book of Lamentations goes on of course, employing a number of rhetorical strategies to express the grief and anger—and, yes, the guilt and repentance—of the community and to elicit a response from God. Chapter 3 shifts to the persona of the "suffering man," who presents a more submissive posture toward God. This male voice makes reference in 3:55–57 to a past in which the divine response was forthcoming:

> I called on your name, O LORD,
>> from the depths of the pit.
> You heard my plea; do not now cover your ear
>> to my cry for help and relief.
> You were near when I called you. You said, "Fear not."

There is never an indication, however, that such a "fear not" is on the present horizon. Even in chapter 3 the dominant tone is one of overwhelming pain and grief. Chapter 4 is closer in imagery and theme to chapters 1 and 2. It too begins with the exclamatory "Alas" (איכה), mixes elements of the dirge with the lament, describes the pitiful state of the ruined city, and mentions the threatened children of Zion (4:2–5). Yet the differences are striking. To begin with, while retaining the acrostic form only two lines are assigned to each letter of the alphabet, rather than the three assigned to each letter in chapters 1 and 2. More significantly, in chapter 4 there are no petitionary elements, no direct address to God, whatsoever. Nor does Zion ever emerge as a speaking subject in Lamentations 4, which consequently allows for no alternating of persona between Zion and the poet. In chapter 5, the final chapter, the acrostic form is missing altogether, though it seems to be reflected in the fact that there are twenty-two lines to the chapter. The chapter represents the purest instance of a communal lament in Lamentations, though the description of misery is unusually long (5:2–18). One finds in chapter 5, for just the briefest of moments, the theme of praise.

> You, O LORD, will reign forever,
>> enthroned from generation to generation. (5:19)

But the flicker of praise is extinguished in the final three verses of the chapter. Here the community speaks in a first-person plural voice, addressing God directly. Lamentations ends with their plaintive appeal:

Why have you forgotten us utterly,
  forsaken us for so long?
Take us back, O LORD, to yourself, and we will come back.
  Renew our days as of old.
For if truly you have rejected us,
  bitterly raged against us . . . (5:20–22)

The final phrase of verse 22 is a poignantly appropriate way to end
the book, inscribing in its near undecidability the very lack of closure represented by God's nonresponse and the poetry's refusal to
move beyond lament. As virtually all commentators note, it is difficult to know how to render the opening Hebrew phrase of 5:22,
כי אם (kî ʾim), which may be literally translated as "for if." Rudolph
argues that it is possible to take the phrase as meaning "unless . . . ,"
implying that the possibility of what follows has been excluded.[48]
But such a use of kî ʾim occurs elsewhere only when preceded by a
clause containing a negative statement. It has also been suggested
that the line be read as a question: "Or have you totally rejected us?
Are you indeed so angry with us?"[49] But there is no evidence in the
Bible of kî ʾim being used to introduce a question, nor is there any
support for taking it to mean "or." Another option, and apparently
that chosen by the Septuagint and the Peshitta (ancient translations
into Greek and Syriac, respectively), is to simply ignore or delete the
particle ʾim, thus rendering line as "for you have truly rejected us,
bitterly raged against us."

   I want to propose here an alternative solution to the problem represented by this verse. It has often been noted that one might expect
the phrase kî ʾim to introduce a conditional statement, but that the
second colon of 5:22 does not seem to state the consequence of the
first as would be expected in a true conditional statement.[50] While
this is true, it does not rule out the conditional nature of kî ʾim. Thus,
I have chosen to translate the line as a conditional statement that is
left trailing off, leaving a protasis without an apodosis, or an "if"
without a "then." The book is left opening out into the emptiness of
God's nonresponse. By leaving a conditional statement dangling, the
final verse leaves open the future of the ones lamenting. It is hardly a
hopeful ending, for the missing but implied apodosis is surely negative, yet it does nevertheless defer that apodosis. And by arresting
the movement from an "if" to a "then" the incomplete clause allows

the reader, for a moment, to imagine the possibility of a different "then," and therefore a different future.

The appeal in 2:20–22, like the appeals made by Zion and the poet in chapters 1 and 2, remains unanswered. The voice of YHWH never sounds in the book of Lamentations; and as Westermann assures, before the move from lament to praise could be made, "first the most important thing had to occur: God's answer."[51] Without such an answer, or perhaps some indication of a salvation oracle, the book of Lamentations remains incomplete. It evidences what Derrida has called a "structural unfinishedness." Nor is this incompletion easily imagined as one that is "carried to term," to return to the epigraph by Edmond Jabès with which I began this chapter. That is, it is not an incompletion that sits well with readers. It is not an incompletion that evokes assent and allows one to move on, as the history of interpretation shows, but is rather "a work that has come only halfway toward its always deferred completion." Though the completion is deferred, its demand is not lessened; Zion's rhetoric of survival remains strong, even if unmet. So reader after reader has attempted to complete the incompletion by filling the void that exists in the place of YHWH's response and by addressing Zion's anguished concern over the fate of her children. Within the borders of Lamentations Zion's children do not survive, but in moving beyond those borders, to the afterlife of this biblical text in other texts, survival becomes possible. And in moving beyond the borders of the book, one moves also from literature of survival to the survival of literature.

THREE

Living beyond Lamentations:
The Rhetoric of Survival in Second Isaiah

> This "survival" does not prolong a life that is already dead;
> it initiates, in the death of what was there, the miracle of
> what is not yet there, of what is not yet identified.
>
> Jean-François Lyotard

> We can grasp some part, at least, of what the survivor's ex-
> perience reveals: that whether felt as a power, or observed
> as a system of activities, life is existence laboring to sustain
> itself, repairing, defending, healing.
>
> Terrence Des Pres

The book of Lamentations ends with absence. It ends with the absence of God and with the absence of survivors. Zion receives no response to her petitions on behalf of her children, the suffering man
of chapter 3 has only the ghosts of salvation oracles past on which to
rely, and the communal voice of chapter 4, waiting "in vain for deliverance," ends in chapter 5 as a community that is forgotten and
forsaken, rejected and raged against. What survival is possible in
such a situation? Any survival in Lamentations would be, in Lyotard's
words, "a miracle of what is not yet there." If there is to be life beyond Lamentations, it must be an initiation of something new in the
death of what was there.

The rhetoric of destruction is overwhelming in the book of
Lamentations; a rhetoric of survival beyond its borders, but rooted
in the book itself, must be likewise overwhelming. Survival in the
wake of such destruction must draw on all its etymological reserves:

"sur-vival" as over-living, as living above, as life in excess. In discussing the survival of literature in belated acts of reading and writing, Jacques Derrida touches on this dynamic:

> We should neither comment, nor underscore a single word, nor extract anything, nor draw a lesson from it. One should not, one should refrain from—such would be the law of the text that gives itself, gives itself up, to be read. Yet it also calls for a violence that matches it in intensity, a violence different in intention, perhaps, but one that exerts itself against the first law only in order to attempt a commitment, an involvement, with that law. To move, yieldingly, towards it, to draw close to it fictively. The violent truth of "reading."[1]

Excessive death is matched by excessive life. Any effort, in Des Pres's words, to sustain, to repair, to heal the life that was poured out in Lamentations will labor "against the first law" even while attempting "a commitment, an involvement" with it. To imagine a healing, a restoration, that is rooted in the rhetoric of destruction found in Lamentations is to imagine a rhetoric of survival that matches it in intensity. The poetry of Second Isaiah takes for itself exactly this task.

The poetry of Lamentations, for all its bleak recognition of rampant destruction, nevertheless maintains a drive—even a demand— for survival. In this chapter I will explore how Second Isaiah (chapters 40–55 in the biblical book of Isaiah) strives to match this drive for survival so prominent in Lamentations. The poetry of Second Isaiah exists in the service of a particular sociohistorical context, namely preparation for the return of exile from Babylon to Judah. The interpretive horizon of this context—including as it does the need for consolation and the buoyant hope of restoration—combines with the violent eloquence of Lamentations to produce a response of an exceedingly positive nature. That is, it is able to hold together the divine response of YHWH and the survival of the children of Zion in a manner that downplays both the notion of Israel suffering on account of its sins and Zion's accusations toward YHWH of excessive brutality.

Previous Treatments of Second Isaiah's Use of Lamentations

Eikhah Rabbah (the primary midrashic commentary on Lamentations) states that "all the severe prophecies that Jeremiah prophesied against Israel were anticipated and healed by Isaiah." For the rabbis, Jeremiah was the author of Lamentations, so the midrash follows the above quotation with responses to each of the twenty-two verses of Lamentations 1, taken from the book of Isaiah. While a modern reader might be inclined to quibble with the details of the responses, or with the assumptions of Jeremianic authorship of Lamentations and the precursive status of the whole book of Isaiah, the insight of the rabbis regarding Second Isaiah's "consciousness of its role as an antidote to the discourse of lamentation"[2] has proved, rather than an exercise in midrashic fancy, to be sound. Not only does Second Isaiah respond to "the discourse of lamentation" in general, but, as it is now becoming clear, to many of the specific verbal formulations of the book of Lamentations itself.

Modern interpreters, like the rabbis, have long noted a similarity of language and theme between Lamentations and Second Isaiah, particularly in the opening call for "comfort" in Isaiah 40:1, but have only rarely and in oblique terms posited a direct relationship. For example, Claus Westermann speculates that Second Isaiah used the root נחם ("comfort/help") in the opening verses, "perhaps on the basis of the lament common in Lamentations, 'There is no helper [מנחם].'"[3] Norman Gottwald reproduces in a footnote a list of verbal linkages provided by Max Löhr and goes so far as to say that Second Isaiah "knew the Book of Lamentations," but he offers no sustained reflection on the significance of this.[4] Carol Newsom advocated a more immediate relationship between the two books in a more recent article:

> What this means is that when Second Isaiah takes up aspects of Lamentations, he engages dialogically the voice of the Judahite community. In Second Isaiah the exiles represent themselves in terms drawn significantly from Judahite speech.[5]

For Newsom, Second Isaiah offers a selective rereading of Lamentations in the service of the exilic community, which is trying to establish a symbolic narrative, based on Judahite discourse, that will allow for the reintegration of exiles into the community that remained in Judah. Newsom construes the symbolic narrative as operating on the basic pattern of reversal, or "antiphonal answering," which matches Isaiah 51:3 with Lamentations 1:2, Isaiah 40:6–8 and 49:1–18 with Lamentations 1:4 and 2:8, Isaiah 52:1 with Lamentations 1:8–10, and Isaiah 49:18 and 51:11 with Lamentations 1:3 and 1:5. The most exhaustive and convincing study of the relationship between the book of Lamentations and Second Isaiah is Patricia Willey's book, *Remember the Former Things*.[6] Willey traces in detail the many citations, allusions, and echoes in Second Isaiah from the Torah, other prophetic books, the Psalms, and Lamentations. Willey's larger argument is that "a driving force of Second Isaiah's rhetoric is the recollection, or re-collection, of other, already familiar texts into its own poetry."[7] Not only did the author of Isaiah 40–55 know and refer to events or traditions, but "particular verbal formulations"[8] of such traditions. She argues that by reusing familiar language Second Isaiah created a discourse at once rooted in tradition and relevant to "a radically altered situation," which is meant to appeal to "a people reevaluating their national self-understanding in the wake of the destruction of their capital city, monarchy, and temple."[9] Willey finds "the most prominent intertextual recollections of Lamentations" in Isaiah 51–52 and "less thoroughgoing but still quite discernible echoes" throughout Isaiah 49–54, both in relation to Daughter Zion and the servant figure.[10] She makes a strong argument that Second Isaiah reflects a knowledge of all five chapters of Lamentations. In this chapter I will explore Second Isaiah's use of Lamentations, in particular as the poetry manifests a concern for the survival of Zion and her children.

Zion in the Context of Second Isaiah

Before looking more closely at the specifics of Zion's and her children's survival in Second Isaiah, it is necessary to look at the structure of Isaiah 40–55 as a whole and to see how the figure of Zion functions within the literary corpus. Although much debate remains concerning whether chapters 40–55 are composed of many short, previously individual, and perhaps oral units, or fewer long and probably originally written poems, there is a consensus among scholars that the final form of chapters 40–55 can be divided into two large sections of 40–48 and 49–55. The first of these sections, after the proclamation that opens the book as a whole in 40:1–11, is primarily concerned either with Babylon or with the exiles from Judah residing in Babylon. The second section, by contrast, is primarily concerned with the two figures of Zion and the servant. The two sections seem to have very different aims and consequently employ different modes of speech and address. The first section employs a rhetoric of release, while the second employs a rhetoric of reintegration. Both are important for how Second Isaiah sets up the imagined homecoming of the exiles and, consequently, for how the book may be seen as a response to Lamentations. After looking briefly at these two sections, I will focus on the figure of Zion and the issues of survival.

The Rhetoric of Release in Isaiah 40–48

Chapters 40–48 address the exiles exclusively as Jacob (nineteen times) and/or Israel (thirty-five times). The terms Zion and Jerusalem occur in these chapters only rarely (a total of eight times), only as an unpersonified city, and never the subject of address.[11] Moreover, only in these chapters is Cyrus mentioned, either by name or allusion, and only here are Babylon or the Chaldeans referred to. The burden of this poetry is to persuade the exiles that YHWH is about to do "a new thing" on their behalf by commissioning Cyrus to conquer Babylon and free YHWH's people.

> Here the prophet's aim is to demonstrate to the people the certainty of the coming release, and to convince them that no obstacles, real or imagined, will avail to hinder their deliverance.[12]

Wilcox and Paton-Williams rightly note that while interpreters often construe this as the message of Second Isaiah as a whole, it is in fact the drive behind chapters 40–48 only.

The poetry of persuasion in these chapters, as numerous commentators have eloquently stated, works mightily to convince its exilic audience of this message. The section is littered with exhortations from YHWH to Jacob/Israel, often in the form of a salvation oracle, which admonishes Jacob/Israel to "fear not, for I am with you" (41:10; see also 41:14; 43:1, 5). All of creation is often called upon to witness to the power of Israel's God to work newness (40:22; 41:18–20; 42:5, 10–12; 43:19–20; 44:3–5, 23–24; 45:8; 48:13). Alternating with these assurances of YHWH's power to rescue the exiles are repeated scenes in which YHWH mocks and ridicules various idols and gods, who can demonstrate no power whatsoever (40:18–20; 41:7, 21–24; 42:8, 17; 43:10–12; 44:9–20; 45:16,

20–21; 46:1–9; 48:5). YHWH, by contrast, is so passionately engaged on behalf of Israel that YHWH rages and roars like a warrior and screams like a woman in labor (42:13–14). All these images and speeches—along with an oratorical style characterized by frequent repetition of key words, the employment of rhetorical questions, and the use of the emphatic Hebrew particle אַף (’ap) no fewer than twenty-five times in nine chapters—combine to undercut the power of Babylon (culminating in chapter 47) and to proclaim the coming exodus of the exiles from it (culminating in chapter 48).

The Rhetoric of Reintegration in Isaiah 49–55

If the focus of chapters 40–48 is on Babylon and is dominated by a rhetoric of persuasion in the service of a new exodus, the focus of chapters 49–55 is on Jerusalem and is dominated by a rhetoric of reintegration in the service of an imagined return of the exiles to their former home. Consequently, the content of chapters 49–55 differs in many ways from the previous section: there is no mention of Babylon or the Chaldeans, no polemic against the idols, no reference to Cyrus, and no address to Jacob/Israel. Instead one finds a frequent use of the terms Jerusalem (five times) and Zion (eight times). Only in this section is Zion personified, portrayed as speaking (49:14), and addressed directly (51:16; 52:7). It is often assumed that "Zion" here represents the exiles or the nation as a whole, and that it is simply a synonym for Jacob/Israel as found in chapters 40–48, but that is not the case. Zion is the city to which the exiled nation is to return. This is consistent with the portrayal of Zion in Lamentations, where the city is described as abandoned, violated, afflicted, in mourning, or under attack. The ones who go into exile, away from Zion, are the citizens of the city (Lam. 1:6, 18; 2:9), often represented as the children of personified Zion (1:5, 1:16), but not Zion herself.[13]

As Newsom has pointed out, one of the main issues of Second Isaiah is how to imagine a homecoming for the exiles after two generations. But just as the message of coming release from bondage is really only a concern of chapters 40–48,[14] so too the issue of a homecoming is really only a concern in chapters 49–55. A geographical shift, from Babylon to Judah, has occurred between the two sections. The first section is closed off with the call in 48:20 for the exiles to depart from Babylon:

> Go out from Babylon,
>   flee from Chaldea!
> Announce with a ringing cry,
>   declare this,
> Send it to the ends of the earth:
>   "The LORD has redeemed his servant Jacob!"

In chapter 49, the movement back to Jerusalem is imagined. YHWH has "answered" the exiles and "helped" them on the day of salvation, in order to restore the land and inherit the "desolate" (Hebrew, שממ; as in Lam. 1:13) heritage (Isa. 49:8). After guiding them through the wilderness in a new "exodus" (49:9–11; cf. 52:12), YHWH announces that the exiles are "coming in from afar" (49:12). Great celebration is expected, for YHWH has "comforted his people" (49:13). The scenario imagined is that the exiles have been freed and have departed from an utterly powerless and humiliated Babylon. They are on the verge of reentering their homeland. The task for the poet now is to finesse the social and ideological problems that might be associated with such a reentry. For this task, the figure of Zion, as the destination for the exiles, becomes all-important.

Survivals of Zion and the "Suffering Man" in Second Isaiah

Because of the strong presence of Zion in chapters 49–55, this section has often been referred to as the Zion/Jerusalem section. While picking up on the importance of the figure of Zion for the latter part of Second Isaiah, such a shorthand reference elides much of the content of these chapters as well as the arrangement of the material. That is, the figure of Zion is matched in 49–55 by the figure of "the servant," with alternating passages focusing first on one and then on the other:[15]

49:1–13	servant section
49:14–50:3	Zion section
50:4–11	servant section
[51:1–8][16]	
51:9–52:12	Zion section
52:13–53:12	servant section
54:1–17	Zion section

The two figures, Zion and the servant of YHWH, are portrayed in similar ways, and as Willey has shown, both of these figures recall in a very detailed manner the respective figures of Zion and the "suffering man" from the book of Lamentations.[17] But just as Zion in Lamentations 1 and 2 is not to be conflated with the male figure of Lamentations 3, neither should the figure of Zion in Second Isaiah be confused with the servant figure.[18] I will not presume to solve here the vexed problem of the identity of the servant figure in Second Isaiah. Innumerable monographs and articles have been written in an attempt to pin down a consistent referent for the "servant of YHWH." There is enough ambiguity preserved in the figure, whether intentionally or not, to ensure that none of the scholarly proposals has been able to command a critical consensus. My primary concern in this chapter, however, is the figure of Zion, especially as it recalls personified Zion from Lamentations. Just as modern interpreters have focused on the suffering man in Lamentations to the virtual exclusion of Zion, so too in Isaiah scholarship the servant figure has claimed an inordinate amount of attention. This is due no doubt to a similar bias toward male figures and especially those that can be construed as a "type" of Jesus. Nevertheless, the close proximity of Zion and the servant and the similarity in their descriptions, both in Lamentations and Second Isaiah, suggest that one should not consider either without at least some reference to the other. Indeed, the servant figure in Second Isaiah is in many ways portrayed as a "survivor." So while my larger study is concerned with the figure of Zion, the servant figure will also be a part of the analysis below.

In attempting to adjudicate the Zion sections and the servant sections of Second Isaiah, it is important to note that in chapters 40–48 the term "servant" is repeatedly and consistently applied to Israel/ Jacob (41:8; 44:1, 2, 21; 45:4; 48:20). There is little doubt that a collective interpretation of the servant figure is warranted in these chapters. But interpreters have tended to consider the so-called servant songs in Isaiah 42:1–7, 49:1–6, 50:4–9, and 52:13–53:12 apart from the surrounding context, allowing the identification of Israel as servant to be obscured. This tendency is based on Bernhard Duhm's original separation, in 1875, of these passages from their literary context, and it is usually supported by the seeming reference in 49:5–6 to the servant as "bringing back" Jacob and "gathering" Israel. If the servant is Israel, so the argument goes, how can the servant also have a mission to Israel? Recent scholarship, however, has

shown the "servant songs" to be much more closely connected to
their literary context than the theory of later interpolation would allow, to the extent that it no longer makes much sense to speak of separate "servant songs" at all.[19] And the problem of the servant having
a mission to Israel disappears when one takes the subject of the in-
finitives in 49:5–6 to be YHWH rather than the servant.[20] Such a decision lies behind the JPSV rendering of Isaiah 49:5:

> And now the LORD has resolved,
> He who formed me in the womb to be His servant,
> to bring back Jacob to Himself,
> that Israel may be restored to Him.
> And I have been honored in the eyes of the LORD,
> my God has been my strength.

It is possible, then, to sustain the interpretation of Israel as servant
into chapters 49–55.

There is a very real difference, however, in how the servant is presented in chapters 49–55 compared with 40–48. In the second half
of the book, the servant is more vividly portrayed as a person, hence
the repeated attempts by scholars to identify a "real" person behind
the portrayal. This is not necessary. What has happened is that the
servant figure has moved from being a collective figure to a personification. While Israel/Jacob represented the collective nation in exile, the
servant is that collective figure "fleshed out" in more detail. That interpreters have been so convinced by the individual portrait witnesses to its effectiveness as a personification. Objections that there
are certain features and descriptions of the servant that do not make
sense in a collective interpretation are not reckoning with the notion
of personification: "If, for instance, Israel is the servant in [the]
fourth song, how does Israel die?"[21] The power of personification is
exactly its ability to posit attributes, actions, etc. to something that
would not otherwise be possible. This is obviously the case with
Zion, personified as a woman in Second Isaiah, but whom no one
imagines must be based on some "real" person.[22]

Taking the servant in Isaiah 49–55 as a personification of Israel has
important implications for how one reads these chapters, particularly
in relation to the book of Lamentations. In the first place, the alternation between the two personified figures pointedly recalls the figures

of Zion and the suffering man of Lamentations. But second, and more important for my own argument, the role of Zion in Second Isaiah, vis-à-vis the servant, emerges more clearly. I claimed above that chapters 49–55 exhibit a rhetoric of reintegration concerning the exiles and the city of Zion. This is true not only for the content of the addresses to Zion (one of which, 49:14–26, I will explore in detail below), but also for the arrangement of the material in these chapters. If one takes the servant to be a personification of Israel, then the alternation between Zion and the servant is a concrete manifestation of the rhetoric of reintegration. The more singular purpose of the poet in chapters 40–48 was reflected in the singular focus on Israel/Jacob, but in 49–55 the dual concerns with both Israel/Jacob and the homeland to which Israel/Jacob is returning are reflected in the alternation between the two figures of Zion and the servant.

While the figures of Zion and the servant are juxtaposed in these chapters, and while they are described with similar language and similar plot lines moving from brokenness to exaltation, they do not overlap or seem aware of each other. The figures run parallel until the very end of the book. At the close of their respective stories the servant and Zion are brought together in an intentional way. In the final Zion poem, Isaiah 54, a glorious restoration of Zion is imagined. YHWH admits to having abandoned Zion, but now swears to be a better husband (54:7–8). While Zion was barren and desolate (54:1), she will now have many children (54:1, 13). At the end of the poem, in 54:17, one finds mention of "the servants of YHWH," only here in explicit connection with Zion: "This is the heritage of YHWH's servants." The desolate heritage, encountered in 49:8, is restored at last to the exiles. As Willey writes:

> The last line addressed to Zion in the book is also the final mention of YHWH's servant. The two parallel motifs are brought together, and the term "servant" is found in plural form for the first and only time, rendering the connection between Zion's children and YHWH's servant finally explicit: YHWH's servants *are* Zion's children, finally returned to their mother city.[23]

The personification of Israel as an individual servant of YHWH falls away now in favor of the plural servants of YHWH. This mirrors a lessening of the personification of Zion in this poem as well. Though

personification is still present to a certain degree—the city is described as a wife and mother—Zion is not used here as a name, and
in verses 11–17 the physical features of a city take over and the "children" of Zion become the servants of YHWH, that is, the returning
exiles. The goal of the poet in Second Isaiah has been met. A way to
imagine the homecoming has been found.

God's Response and the Restoration of Zion's Children in Isaiah 49:14–26

While the figure of Zion is important for understanding the larger
rhetorical and ideological project represented by Second Isaiah, the
most striking correspondences between the book of Lamentations
and Second Isaiah may be seen in the details of the text. More particularly, in Isaiah 49:14–26 the two lingering issues that I have
identified as most important in Lamentations 1 and 2 are explicitly
addressed: the absent response of YHWH to Zion is here provided,
and the children of Zion who were lost are here returned.

Providing the Response of YHWH

That YHWH's response in this poem is meant as an answer to the in-
dictments of Lamentations is indicated from the start.

> Zion said:
> > The LORD has abandoned me,
> > my Lord has forgotten me. (Isa. 49:14)

This, the opening of the poem, is nearly a direct quote from Lamentations 5:20:

> Why have you forgotten us forever,
> > abandoned us without end?

The same word pair, "forgotten" and "abandoned" (שכח and עזב),
is picked up by the poet of Second Isaiah and placed in the mouth of
Zion as a prelude to YHWH's extended response that follows. If one
wants to know where Zion said this, one need only turn to Lamentations 5:20.[24] The recollection of this word pair is not easily explained as a coincidence. Although the words are, separately, quite
common in the Hebrew Bible, they occur together only rarely and
never elsewhere with YHWH as the subject who "forgets" and "aban-

dons."[25] While there seems to be little doubt that the reference here is to Lamentations 5:20, it is not quite a direct quote. First, Zion, to whom the complaint is attributed in Second Isaiah, is not in fact the speaker in Lamentations 5:20. The personified figure of Zion occurs only in chapters 1 and 2 of the book of Lamentations; the question of 5:20 occurs in the context of a communal lament, spoken in the first-person plural. But in the exilic milieu of Second Isaiah, Zion dominates the horizon of Judah. All Judahite speech has been subsumed under the figure of personified Zion. As Newsom has shown, this not a disinterested move. By eliding the voices of the Judahite community, the poet can more easily imagine a homecoming for the exiles. What was once a complaint of the people who remained in Jerusalem after the destruction becomes a complaint of personified Zion, which, as will be clear below, is answered not by addressing the complaint of the Judahite community but by restoring Zion's exiled "children."

Given the aims of the poetry identified above, this co-opting of Judahite discourse on behalf of the exilic community is to be expected. The voice of the Judahites, represented by Lamentations, "survives" in Second Isaiah, but it is not simply reproduced there. And even if it were "reproduced," it could not remain unchanged. Here I return to Walter Benjamin, who wrote in his essay "The Work of Art in the Age of Mechanical Reproduction":

> Even the most perfect reproduction of a work of art is lacking in one element: its presence in time and space, its unique existence at the place where it happens to be.[26]

When one takes into account its "presence in time and space," even the reproduction is transformed. "In permitting the reproduction to meet the beholder or listener in his own particular situation, it reactivates the object reproduced."[27] In the poetry of Second Isaiah, which indeed very nearly reproduces Lamentations 5:20, the communal complaint is reactivated in the service of a particular situation. In its context in Lamentations, the word pair "forget" and "abandon" occurred at the end of five chapters of nearly unrelieved complaint. As an unanswered question, Lamentations 5:20 reinforced the felt absence of God's voice that Zion had inscribed so acutely in chapters 1 and 2. (Hence, its association with Zion in Second Isaiah.) Combined

with the near untranslatable trailing off of 5:22, "For if truly you have
rejected us / bitterly raged against us . . . ,"[28] this unanswered question epitomizes the lack of closure in Lamentations. Derrida's comments on Maurice Blanchot's novella *L'arrêt de mort* are appropriate:
"But how are we to decide, to fix the end of such a text? Its unfinishedness is structural; it is bound to itself in the shifting binding of
the *arrêt*."[29] The poetry of Second Isaiah can be taken as just such an
attempt to "fix" the end of Lamentations by providing the answer to
just this unanswered question. It is significant also that in its "survival" in Isaiah 49:14, the question of Lamentations 5:20 is transformed into a statement. The poet of Second Isaiah knows well the
power of a rhetorical question to grasp and hold the hearer or reader.
It is one of the poet's favorite literary techniques, and here it is reserved for YHWH (Isa. 49:15). Moreover, by turning the question into
a perfect-tense statement, its "pastness" is emphasized: what may
have been true in the past (cf. 54:7–8) is in any case no longer true.

The Return of Zion's Children

While it is of great importance that YHWH is portrayed as answering
Zion, what is even more striking is the content of YHWH's response.
For what follows Zion's statement of abandonment and forgottenness in Isaiah 49:14 are eleven verses pertaining almost exclusively
to the return of the children that Zion had lost.

  This return of Zion's children represents the poet's attempt to por-
tray YHWH as giving Zion the "comfort" that was so lacking in
Lamentations. The first of many descriptions in Lamentations of Zion
having "none to comfort her" occurs in 1:9b. On the heels of that
statement, Zion breaks in with the imperative, "See, O LORD, my suffering (עניי)" (1:9c). But in Lamentations, YHWH apparently does not
see and definitely does not comfort. In Isaiah 49:13, however, it is
said that YHWH has comforted (נחם) YHWH's people and shown
mercy (רחם) to YHWH's afflicted ones (עניו). Willey has seen that this
is almost certainly an echo of Lamentations 1. But I disagree with her
judgment that Zion's statement of abandonment and forgottenness in
49:14 is meant to show an inattentiveness to all that YHWH has been
described as doing in chapters 40–48 and into 49:1–13.[30] The description of YHWH's comfort for the afflicted ones in 49:13 in fact has
nothing to do with Zion, but rather with "YHWH's people," that is

those in exile. I noted above that this statement comes at the end of an announcement of release for the Judahite exiles in Babylon and that it brings them to the verge of a homecoming. Zion's status as "afflicted one" and her need for "comfort" have both been transferred to the exiles, which are not to be confused with Zion. Therefore, Zion's statement in 49:14 is not incongruent with all that comes before it. Rather, it fits quite well with the emphasis on the exiles and the geographic location of Babylon that pervades Isaiah 40–48. It is Zion's complaint in 49:14 that marks the point of transition to Jerusalem. Zion has remained, in the ideology of Second Isaiah if not in reality, abandoned and forgotten, and this condition will be addressed precisely by the return of Zion's children, i.e., the exiles. The two have been linked by the application of Zion's earlier complaint to the exiles (49:13), who will now be (as Zion's children) the means of answering Zion's quite legitimate complaint in Isaiah 49:14.

In order to answer Zion's complaint, YHWH begins by assuming the persona of a mother (49:15):

> Can a woman forget her nursing child?
> Or have no pity for the child of her womb?
> Even these may forget,
> but I will not forget you.

The acknowledgment that "even these may forget" is perhaps an allusion to Lamentations 2:20, where women in the siege of Jerusalem do indeed show no pity and cannibalize their children. In any case, the poet chooses here the one metaphor for YHWH that can begin to answer the rhetoric of Lamentations: YHWH as a mother who also laments and hopes for the return of her children. In the extended response from YHWH that follows, there are numerous echoes of the language and themes of Lamentations, particularly chapters 1 and 2. Given the poem's role as a response to Zion's laments, the focus remains squarely on the restoration of Zion's lost children, with whom she was so concerned in Lamentations. For example, in Lamentations 1:5 and 1:16 children are juxtaposed with enemies.

> Her sucklings have gone into captivity
> before the enemy. (1:5c)
> My children are ravaged,
> for the enemy has triumphed. (1:16c)

In Isaiah 49:17 one finds a similar juxtaposition. But while in
Lamentations the children went into exile at the coming of the enemies (1:5), in Isaiah the children return and the former "destroyers
and devastators" are made to "go out" from Zion.

In Lamentations 1 and 2, however, Zion's children are not only described as going into exile but also as being murdered by sword (1:20;
2:21) and slaughtered without pity (2:21), as dying in the squares of
the city (2:11) and in the arms of their mothers (2:12), and as being
cannibalized both by the enemy (2:22) and by their mothers (2:20).
The image of death and bereavement is finally more pervasive in
Lamentations—which is, after all, about the destruction of the city—
than is the image of children going into exile. Although it is much
more difficult to imagine the restoration of dead children than it is to
imagine the returning of children from exile, the poetry of Second Isaiah does not shy away from the task. Zion is told in 49:20:

> The children of your bereavement
>   shall yet say in your hearing:
> "The place is too crowded for me,
>   make room for me to settle."

The children of Zion's bereavement (בני שכליך) are those children
who were murdered or who died in the streets. Translations typically
elide the meaning of the Hebrew word used here to indicate bereavement (שכל) by rendering the phrase as "the children you
thought you had lost" (JPSV), or "children born in the time of your
bereavement" (NRSV), or even "the children which thou shalt have,
after thou hast lost the other" (KJV). But in the Hebrew Bible the
word everywhere and always means to suffer the death of one's children, as in Zion's statement in Lamentations 1:20:

> Outside, the sword bereaves.
> Inside, there is death.

The translations are trying to explain something that is beyond explanation. But the poet is proclaiming what the sixteenth-century
Polish poet Jan Kochanowski, in his laments (Treny) over the death of
his young daughter, could only imagine:

> Wherever you may be—if you exist—
> Take pity on my grief. O presence missed,

Comfort me, haunt me; you whom I have lost,
Come back again, be shadow dream, or ghost.[31]

The poet does not imagine that by some sort of trickery Zion's children were never in fact dead ("does not prolong a life that is already
dead"),[32] but rather claims that those children who were dead are now
alive ("it initiates, in the death of what was there, the miracle of what
is not yet there").[33] Moreover, the survival imagined here is not just a
"life after death," but "more life or more than life, and better":[34] "those
other meanings that rework 'living on' or 'surviving' (*super, hyper,* 'over,'
über, and even 'above' and 'beyond')."[35] For a certain rhetorical giddi-
ness sets in, as the poet compounds the image of restoration to the point
that there is not even room enough for all the restored children.

Zion's response confirms this sense of survival as "overliving."
She can only repeat to herself in stunned amazement:

Who bore these for me?
    I was bereaved and desolate.[36]
Who brought these up?
    See how I was left alone.
These, where were they? (49:21)

Zion's disbelief at the news of their return is understandable. Such
a thing is unimaginable. But the rhetoric of survival is strong in Second Isaiah, for it must attempt to succeed the rhetoric of destruction
in Lamentations. The chapter ends with a final affirmation of YHWH's
resolve to answer Zion's formerly unanswered laments. As in the beginning of YHWH's speech (49:15), the poet employs a rhetorical
question:

Can the spoil be taken from a warrior,
    or captives recovered from a tyrant?[37]
Yet thus says the LORD:
Captives will be taken from a warrior,
    and spoil will be recovered from a tyrant.
For I will contend with your contenders,
    and I will rescue your children. (49:24–25)

The theme of reversal and restoration is served in this passage by a
subtle rhetoric of reversal. A complex pattern structures the first part
of the passage:

    a) taken/warrior/spoil   b) captives/tyrant/recovered
                        c) thus says YHWH
    d) captives/warrior/taken   e) spoil/tyrant/recovered

While the verbs and indirect objects exist in a parallel relationship in
which "a" matches up with "d," and "b" matches up with "e," the
subjects each colon are reversed in a chiastic pattern in which "a"
matches up with "e," and "b" matches up with "d." The theme of
reversal carries over to 49:25c, where those who once contended
with Zion will now be contended with by YHWH, and Zion's children (the captives of verses 24 and 25) will now be set free. The reversal of Zion's fortunes is complete in the chapter's final verse
(49:26), where it is said that Zion's oppressors "will eat their own
flesh" (i.e., offspring; cf. Isa. 58:9). We may recall that this same
trope of the horrors of a besieged city was used in the book of
Lamentations.

The Terms of Survival in Second Isaiah

Zion in Second Isaiah is portrayed in ways consistent with her portrayal in the book of Lamentations. There are very real differences
between the two figures as well, owing to different sociohistorical
contexts and rhetorical concerns of the two texts. As a response to
overwhelming destruction—both of physical structures and structures of meaning—Zion emerges in Lamentations as an emphatic
speaking subject, who repeatedly uses the imperative in addressing
YHWH (1:9c, 11c, 20; 2:20). She voices an insistent demand for
YHWH to see the destruction and to act to save her children. Zion in
Lamentations represents a voice of survival and for survival: she is
herself a survivor and she seeks the survival of her children. At the
same time, it is clear that the horizon of Lamentations, while demanding survival, was unable to imagine survival as a live option. Zion
receives no answer from YHWH, and she must admit that of all her
children "none survived or escaped on the day of YHWH's wrath"
(2:22). As Benjamin writes: "One of the foremost tasks of art has always been the creation of a demand that can only be satisfied later."[38]
The poet of Second Isaiah is aware of his task to try to satisfy a demand that was created earlier.

    In Second Isaiah, both the figure of Zion and the issue of survival are still in the foreground. But now matters are reversed. While Zion spoke much in Lamentations and YHWH was silent, in Second Isaiah Zion speaks little and YHWH proves positively loquacious. In contrast to Lamentations, it is now YHWH who addresses imperatives to Zion (Isa. 49:18; 51:17; 52:1). And while Zion vigorously intercedes on behalf of her perishing children in Lamentations, in Second Isaiah YHWH vigorously declares that the children who had perished are now returning to Zion. Zion's role now has changed from a parent fighting tooth and nail for the survival of her children to a parent welcoming back children who have in fact survived. Patricia Willey is certainly right in her observation that while the poetry of Second Isaiah means to answer and redress the concerns of Zion in Lamentations, it does so at the expense of Zion's strident subjectivity:

> She is no longer a subject to act, but an object awaiting the actions of others . . . Though told to rise up and put on her strength, she no longer displays the strength she showed in Lamentations.[39]

The figure of Zion from Lamentations has been co-opted to serve a role in the ideology of Second Isaiah; but the figure of Zion has also set the terms for the imagined restoration. Her demand for the survival of her children has contributed as much to the poetry of Second Isaiah as has the ideology behind the exiles' return.

At stake in Isaiah 49:14–26, from beginning to end, is the survival of children. Metaphorically, of course, the poem is concerned with the survival of the nation of Judah. The poet discerned and responded to the need for a rhetoric of survival generated by Lamentations, and he utilized this response to articulate an ideology of survival generated by the social context. Thus, the leading metaphor of "survival" holds together two connotations of one of the primary Hebrew terms for "children" (בנים): the innocence and utter helplessness of the children, and the notion that any future for Judah as a nation resides precisely in these threatened ones.

FOUR

Survival in Translation:
The Targum to Lamentations

The original requires translation even if no translator is
there, fit to respond to this injunction, which is at the same
time demand and desire in the very structure of the original. This structure is the relation of life to survival.

                                                    Jacques Derrida

In its survival—which would not merit the name if it were
not mutation and renewal of something living—the original is modified.

                                                    Walter Benjamin

If the book of Lamentations ends with the absence of God and the
absence of Zion's children, Second Isaiah ends with the full (one
might even say overfull) restoration of both. The answer from God
that Zion demanded crowds the chapters of Second Isaiah, and the
children she lamented, the children of her bereavement, crowd the
desolate places. The antiphonal response of Second Isaiah endeavors
to match the intensity of complaint with an equal intensity of response. The poet imagines to have filled the lack that confronts the
reader of Lamentations.

The irony of Second Isaiah's attempt to answer the language of
death and absence in Lamentations, to counter it with the language
of survival, is that it threatens the very life of Lamentations as literature. The "potentially eternal afterlife" of the work of art about
which Walter Benjamin writes depends on a "demand and desire"
that cannot be easily nullified.[1] Writing about the "unfinishedness"

of a text that "overruns all the limits assigned to it," Jacques Derrida concedes that such a de-bordement (or "overflowing") "will still have come as a shock, producing endless efforts to dam up, resist, rebuild the old partitions."[2] Second Isaiah's antiphonal response to Lamentations may be taken as just such an effort to dam up the torrent of rage (on the part of God), death (on the part of the children), and tears (on the part of Mother Zion) that "pour out" from the book.[3]

The effort of Second Isaiah to counter the overrun of Lamentations, to establish the outer edge of its reach, is at most partly successful. This effort, as shown in the previous chapter, was in the service of a particular ideology for a particular social and historical context, and it consequently took a form appropriate to that context. However, the response of Second Isaiah was generated not only by its own sociohistorical context, but also by the "original" to which it responds, the book of Lamentations itself. Despite the forceful nature of its rhetoric of survival, Second Isaiah does not answer Lamentations once and for all, though the poet may have wished to do so for his own generation. The "demand and desire in the very structure of the original" of which Derrida writes in the epigraph to this chapter, though generative of those attempts to meet them, are finally independent of such attempts. This is, Derrida claims, "the relation of life to sur-vival." Recall Benjamin's description of the "vital connection" between a text and its translation:

> Just as the manifestations of life are intimately connected with life itself without signifying anything for it, a translation issues from the original—not so much from its life as from its "afterlife."[4]

As a "survival" of Lamentations, the poetry of Second Isaiah participates in its afterlife, but does not affect the "life" of the original to which it responds. Regarding the book of Lamentations, to borrow Derrida's description of Blanchot's novella, "[w]hat must remain beyond its reach is precisely what revives it at every moment."[5] The survival that is lacking in the literature is what ensures the survival of Lamentations as literature. The demand of Zion for her children's survival and the reader's desire to meet that demand, which may potentially come together every time the biblical book is read, draw attention to the lack that remains in the original and thereby ensure that survival remains very much a live issue in the history of interpretation.

The book of Lamentations remains, and so remains its voicing of the plight of children and its utter lack of consolation. Thus, in other interpretive contexts than Second Isaiah's, one may expect the book of Lamentations to exert no less powerful an influence on those texts that survive it. And while the need for a response to Zion's appeal will stay prominent in this interpretive afterlife, it will be met in differing ways according to different sociohistorical horizons. The next scene in the drama of the afterlife of Lamentations may be found in Targum Lamentations (an Aramaic translation from late antiquity), wherein one can explore another attempt to address the concerns of Mother Zion.

The Nature and Character of Targum

Before looking at the specifics of the response to Zion in Targum Lamentations, it will be useful to explore the character of targum in general and, in particular, how it relates to Walter Benjamin's notion of translation as survival.

Targum as Translation

It is routine among scholars to describe the essential nature of targum as "translation." Indeed, the word targum (plural targumim) itself derives from the quadrilateral Semitic root תרגם, which carries the basic sense of "to translate." The root seems to be used in this sense in its only biblical occurrence (Ezra 4:7), and in rabbinic Hebrew the pi'el form of the verb (תירגם, tîrgēm) means to translate the Bible from Hebrew into a second language, usually Aramaic but at times Greek (y. Qiddushin 59a; y. Megillah 71c). In modern scholarship, however, the term "targum" is used in a restricted sense to refer to a translation of the Hebrew Bible into Aramaic. Targum may refer to either the practice of translation that took place in ancient synagogues, or the literary documents that preserve actual Aramaic versions of biblical books. In a standard survey of the history of Jewish literature, Meyer Waxman expresses well the common explanation for the origins of targum:

> With the return of the Jews from Babylon, there began the spread of Aramaic in Palestine as a spoken language, or as a vernacular, . . . [and] under the circumstances there arose a need for the use of the Aramaic in the teaching and the interpretation of the Bible to the people.[6]

According to the Mishnah (m. Megillah 4:4), the translation into Aramaic was made in tandem with the reading from the Hebrew original, with no pause between the two. There were strict rabbinic rules on the practice of targum, including the stipulation that while the Hebrew must always be read, the targum was always to be recited orally. Targum belonged to the Oral Torah (תורה שבעל-פה), and was always to be distinguished from the Written Torah (תורה שבכתב).[7]

There are, however, problems with the accepted account of the origins and function of targum. First, the prohibition on reducing targumim to writing raises the question of how the targum as document began and what function it may have had. Second, explaining the origin of targum as institution in terms of a simple need to communicate the Hebrew Bible to speakers of Aramaic fails to explain why the practice of targum persisted even after Aramaic was replaced by Arabic as the vernacular. Third, even the basic sense of targum as a "translation" at all has come under challenge, given the seeming liberties that the targum takes in adding to and explaining the biblical material.

Alexander Samely has addressed these issues in an important way in his book The Interpretation of Speech in the Pentateuch Targums. Samely writes:

> The assessment that the original rationale of oral targum was very likely a translation need and its Sitz im Leben the synagogal Bible lesson, together with the fact that written targums happen to be in Aramaic, has effectively channeled the literary form of targum in the direction of translation.[8]

Samely challenges the assumption that targum should be understood as belonging to the genre of translation on two counts. First, he holds that "there is no other translational text in Jewish antiquity (or, as far as I am aware, outside it) that shares the peculiar features of targum," and that there is no ancient theory of translation to account for it.[9] Second, he raises the very cogent point that to call translation a "genre" (as scholars are wont to do in regard to targum) is to obscure the fact that the text to be translated, rather than the existence of the targum as translation, determines the question of genre. Samely himself prefers to call targum "Aramaic paraphrase." While I find much of Samely's argument convincing, I am less content than he to be rid of the word "translation" in reference to targum. As Samely admits, although the targum does indeed add much to the original text, it does this in addition to, not instead of, translating it.[10] Additions are made between sentences, between phrases, and even between words, yet they virtually never replace the original words or their sequence. So while targum is in fact translation, it is not "merely" translation. As I will argue below, the targum is an extraordinary example of Walter Benjamin's notion of translation as survival.

Targum as Exegesis

It is also routine among scholars to agree that the targumim as we have them preserve much more than what is commonly thought of as translation. In fact, the verbal form tîrgēm in rabbinic Hebrew may also mean to "explain" or "interpret" a biblical verse or a mishnah in the same language as the original text. So while targum can be rightly described as translation, it can also be rightly described as interpretation. Having said that targum is or contains interpretation as well as translation, one must inquire how the two are related and, furthermore, what sort of interpretation the targumim represent. Such an inquiry is most commonly done in terms of "explanation." That is, scholars have assumed that the primary task of the meturgeman (the reciter of targum) was to impart information to the hearer, and so was "prepared to introduce into the translation as much interpretation as seemed necessary to clarify the sense."[11] Sperber argues that targum was intended to make the Scriptures available to "the less educated classes," and so it was primarily concerned with "clarity of expression" in order that "the listener or the reader does not have to exert his intelligence" to understand the Bible.[12]

While this line of reasoning may account for some aspects of targum, it cannot explain the material in targum that so obviously does not serve simply to explain or clarify, but in fact often makes the targum a much more complicated document than the original. Consequently, the theory of targumic interpretation as explanation must exclude such material from what is essential to targum. This is done by calling this material "aggadic [midrashic or interpretive] embellishment,"[13] and thus equating it with midrash (explained in chapter five) rather than targum, or by simply dismissing those targumim with a preponderance of such material as not genuine targum at all.

As Waxman writes: "The versions to the Five Scrolls [Song of Songs, Ruth, Lamentations, Ecclesiastes, and Esther] are really no translations but homiletic Midrashim."[14] Even those scholars who admit that the more expansive material is not alien to targum nevertheless tend to see no intrinsic connection between the interpretations offered by the targumim and the material that they translate. Consider Etan Levine's statement in his introduction to Targum Lamentations:

> To make the biblical text more understandable, acceptable, relevant or polemical, midrash or midrashic allusion was woven into the translation, forming a continuous reading, without distinction between translation, alteration and addition.[15]

Although Levine argues strongly that the expansive material in Targum Lamentations should be considered original to it, that is, not a later interpolation, he nevertheless does not view it as either related to the biblical text or intrinsic to the character of targum. The material is "midrashic" and, since it exists as clarification or polemic, is primary related to the horizon of the *meturgeman* rather than the biblical text.

I am once again in agreement with Alexander Samely, who argues against the consensus that targum is fundamentally "exegetical" in nature. After a thorough investigation of Pseudo-Jonathan, Samely concludes that "exegetical preoccupations set the topic both for apparently narrative additions and theological statements."[16] Although the targumim undoubtedly contain theological and polemical material that reflects rabbinic ideological concerns, the same material can also be considered and studied as exegesis of the original Hebrew text; the one does not preclude the other. Before considering below how the targumic expansions concerning Zion and her children exist in an exegetical relationship to the biblical text of Lamentations, I will first address briefly the appropriateness of understanding targum in terms of "survival."

Targum as Survival

While the categories of translation and exegesis are able to comprehend certain aspects of targum and the targumim, neither alone is able to account for targum as a whole. I suggested above that targum is an extraordinary example of Walter Benjamin's description of translation in terms of survival. I intend in this section to make clear what I mean by that and to show that taking targum as "survival," as a manifestation of the "afterlife" of a biblical text, accounts for the disparate aspects of targumic literature that have so vexed the attempts to categorize it.

In "The Task of the Translator" Benjamin writes the following concerning translation:

> For in its survival—which would not merit the name if it were not the mutation and renewal of something living—the original is modified. Even for the firmly established word there is still a postmaturation.[17]

The two words that Benjamin uses here to describe what he means by survival, "mutation" and "renewal," correspond well to the two aspects of targum identified above: renewal being the essence of translation, and mutation capturing well the exegetical bent of targum. The targumim as translations allow for the original texts to be "renewed" in a new context and for a new audience. In Benjamin's words, "their translation marks their stage of continued life." In one sense, this is not so very different from the standard description of targum as translation. Except that Benjamin is adamant that translation, or at least what he deems to be "good" translation, does not concern itself with the imparting of information or even with the audience at all, which is the hallmark of the traditional scholarly view of targum. According to Benjamin, this would be to transmit only "something inessential" to the original. "If the original does not exist for the reader's sake, how could the translation be understood on the basis of this premise?"[18] Since the work of art or literature is unconcerned either to impart information or to address its audience ("No poem is intended for the reader, no picture for the beholder, no symphony for the listener") but rather strives toward something it lacks, a good translation exists simply because the original "calls for it."[19] Translation is renewal, but a renewal driven not by the demand of an audience but rather by the demand of the original.

Benjamin's typically overreaching formulation of the problem likely needs to be nuanced; yet he provides the concepts and terminology by which to articulate a more complex understanding of targum. The targumim surely exist as a sort of "mutation" of the original. Not only does the original experience a renewed life, but a life that is significantly different from its previous form. For the modern reader with the biblical and targumic texts of Lamentations side by side, it may be that the "mutation" represented by the targum—its expansions of dialogue, direct address to the audience, and interpretive material—in rendering the "original" precludes it from even being called a translation. It must be kept in mind, however, that the targumim were never meant to replace an original text, but rather were produced "in tandem" with the Hebrew verses they translated and took place before an attentive and critical audience. As Avigdor Shinan notes, "the proximity of the Hebrew scriptural verse was crucial."[20] The issue becomes, then, not whether or not targum is a mutation of the original, but to what extent this mutation is a part of the original's striving toward what it lacks. As I will show below, the expansions in Targum Lamentations concerning Zion and her children are not unrelated to the biblical text and are not just polemic or explanation geared for the text's new audience. Rather, they exist in an *exegetical* relationship to the biblical text as part of an interpretive afterlife generated by the original text. Commenting on Benjamin's essay on translation, Derrida writes:

> If the translator neither restitutes nor copies an original, it is because the original lives on and transforms itself. The translation will truly be a moment in the growth of the original, which will complete itself in enlarging itself. Now, it has indeed to be, and it is in this that the "seminal" logic must have imposed itself on Benjamin, that growth not give rise to just any form in just any direction. Growth must accomplish, fill, complete.[21]

If what Derrida writes is true for the targum, that its excesses come about because "the original calls for a complement,"[22] and if my reading of the "original" Lamentations is correct, that it is driven by a concern for the suffering of children, then one may presume a confluence of the two claims. In other words, does the targum exhibit "growth" along the trajectory of "concern for children"? The answer is yes, as the following discussion of Targum Lamentations will show.

The Nature and Character of Targum Lamentations

Targum Lamentations exists in two recensions: the Western Text and the Yemenite Text. Western Text manuscripts were written in Europe and North Africa, but their origins are generally thought to be Palestinian.[23] The relationship between the two recensions is not clear, though it appears that in many cases the Yemenite Text offers a truncated version of the Western Text.[24] Any influence from one recension to another, however, should be considered late. Philip Alexander, after a detailed comparison of the two recensions of Targum Lamentations, concludes:

> The two families of texts cannot be stemmatically related to each other, nor should the procedures of classical text criticism be applied to recover a common Urtext behind them. West. cannot be derived mechanically from Yem. as it stands, or vice versa. The variations are large, widespread and systematic, and, therefore, recensional.[25]

Owing to its superior linguistic coherence, the Yemenite Text has been given more attention by philologists and has been the basis of two modern critical editions, those of Sperber and van der Heide.[26] The Western Text has been used for only one modern edition, that of Levine, which has been severely criticized by other scholars for its general sloppiness.[27] But with regard to the substance (as opposed to linguistic coherence) of the recension, the Western Text is superior. "There can be no doubt that if we are concerned with the aggadic content of the Targum, then our starting-point must be the western recension."[28] Since the aggadic content is my main concern in this chapter, I will utilize the Western Text in the discussion below, referring to the Yemenite tradition when appropriate.

As with the practice of targum in general, in Targum Lamentations the aggadic material is interwoven with the original text, thus producing what often seems like a completely new literature, while nevertheless maintaining a near lexical equivalent for every word in the original. The aggadic additions in Targum Lamentations occur almost exclusively in chapters 1 and 2.[29] In chapters 3–5 of the targum one finds nearly a word-for-word rendering of the Hebrew into Aramaic, with only one genuine expansion (in 3:28; to which I will return below). Previous studies concerned with the theological implications of Targum Lamentations have tended to focus on the expansions to the opening verses of chapter 1, where the theme of Israel's sin is quite prevalent. In this section of the targum, one finds two major blocks of midrashic material that emphasize a history of sinfulness. The fourth petihta (proem, or introductory comments;

plural *petihtaot*) of the midrash to Lamentations, which connects the opening word, "Alas" (איכה, pronounced *'êkah*), of Lamentations 1:1 with God's question to Adam in Genesis 3, "Where are you?" (איכה, pronounced *'ayyekah*), is utilized to compare the exile of Judah with the banishment from Eden. A comment on Numbers 14:1, recounting how God decided to allow the temple to be destroyed on the Ninth of Av because that was the day that Israel wept in response to the negative report brought back by the spies sent to Canaan, is inserted into verse 2.[30] According to the targum, Israel was given the opportunity by Jeremiah to repent but did not do so and the destruction was carried out.

By focusing on these expansions to the opening verses, and by arguing that they set the tone for all that follows, scholars have construed Targum Lamentations as a monolithic document that can be read only as advocating an acceptance of suffering as "punishment [that] was deserved for acting against God's will."[31] As was the case with biblical Lamentations, however, this is simply too reductive of a reading of the targum text. In the following section, I will focus on the expansions explicitly connected to the figure of Zion and her children, which have tended to be excluded from discussions of the theological *Tendenz* of the targum. But in doing so, I will demonstrate that Targum Lamentations participates in the exegetical trajectory that I have identified in the history of interpretation. I will also argue that Targum Lamentations offers a more complex and conflicted attitude toward suffering than is usually acknowledged by those interpreters who characterize it as an unwavering voice of orthodoxy.

Zion and Her Children in Targum Lamentations

In my reading of Lamentations in chapter two above, I identified a number of key verses in the biblical text where Zion focused on the survival of her children. Three of these verses were 1:16, 2:20, and 2:22. It is significant that at these verses in particular Targum Lamentations evinces a desire to supplement the biblical text, and it is quite telling to notice how it goes about making these supplements. I will look closely at each of these verses in Targum Lamentations in comparison with the original in the Masoretic text of Lamentations, and then conclude this chapter with a consideration of the theological implications of these supplements.

Lamentations 1:16

Lamentations 1:16 was a crucial verse for my reading of the Masoretic text of Lamentations in chapter two, since here Zion is first presented as overcome with emotion on behalf of her abused children. The biblical text of 1:16 reads:

> For these things I weep . . . My eyes, my eyes!
>   They stream with tears.
> How far from me is one to comfort,
>   one to restore my life.
> My children are ravaged;
>   the enemy has triumphed.

Zion's initial accusation against God (combined with elements of the description of pain) in 1:11c–16 culminates with this emphasis on children, an emphasis that becomes even clearer in Lamentations 2. But given the other motifs present in this first speech of Zion, one might understandably equivocate on my claim for the preeminence of the children here. In fact, Claus Westermann takes the phrase "for these things" (על אלה) to refer back to the previous material rather than to what follows in 1:16. He even argues that 16c "exhibits no meaningful connection" with its surrounding context.[32] To read 1:16 as Westermann does obviously undercuts much of the emphasis on the survival of Zion's children that I identified as coming into focus here. The targum's version of 1:16, however, explicitly reinforces such an emphasis on children. It reads:

> Because of the babes who were smashed and the pregnant women whose wombs were torn open, the Congregation of Israel says, "I weep, and my eyes pour out tears like a spring of waters. Look how far from me is any comforter to revive me and to give my life consolation. Oh, how my children are desolate, look how the enemy has triumphed over them."[33]

While the targum makes some typical minor changes, such as rendering "my eye, my eye" as "my eyes"[34] and identifying Zion as "the Congregation (כנשתא) of Israel," the most significant change is the addition of the two italicized phrases.[35] While the biblical text reads only "because of these things I weep," mentioning the children at the end of the verse, the targum supplements this with the first additional phrase "Because of the babes who were smashed and the pregnant women whose wombs were torn open." The cause of Zion's breakdown, which I identified as the fate of the children, is picked up by the targum as a point of supplementarity. By presenting the children as "smashed" and "torn" from their mothers' wombs, the targum intensifies the emotional level. And by having the fate of the children at the beginning and end of the verse, thus forming an *inclusio*, it emphasizes their importance as the cause of Zion's (or Congregation of Israel's) weeping.

Perhaps too much should not be made of the presence of the second additional phrase, which I have rendered as "and to give my life consolation" (וממלל תנחומין על נפשי). It is missing from all the manuscripts of the Yemenite recension, but its presence in the Western Text adds one key theme to the verse. A more literal translation of the Aramaic phrase would be "to speak consolation over my life." Thus, the addition of this phrase connects comfort with speech. This was also a key theme in chapter 2 of Lamentations, where the poet calls attention to his task of trying to find words adequate to express Zion's pain, that he might comfort (נחם; 2:13) her in some way. (And it perhaps reflects a recognized connection between Lamentations and Isaiah 40:1–2.) The targum intuits the need for a response to Zion's accusations already in 1:16. The theme becomes more central and unmistakable in the next major supplement to biblical Lamentations that I will consider, Targum Lamentations 2:20.

Lamentations 2:20

Another crucial passage for my reading of Lamentations was Zion's final speech of 2:20–22, in which she responds to the exhortation of the poet to affront God with the suffering of the children in order to elicit a response. The text of 2:20 reads:

> Look, O LORD, and pay attention to whom it is
> you have so ruthlessly afflicted!
> Alas! Women are eating their offspring,
> the children they have borne!
> Behold how priest and prophet are slain
> in the sanctuary of the LORD.

In my reading of the passage in chapter two above, I suggested that
those whom YHWH has "so ruthlessly afflicted" are the children of the
line immediately following. Noting the recurrence of the image of
children at the end of 2:22, I argued that the image of children served
as a symbolic condensation for the figures of "priest and prophet,
youth and maiden" that came between the two verses. The image of
children bracketed the description of the inhabitants of the city.

The targum to Lamentations makes a number of significant
changes in 2:20 compared with the Masoretic text:

> Look O LORD and pay attention from *heaven*: Whom have you afflicted like
> these? Is it right that *from starvation* the daughters of Israel should eat the
> fruit of their wombs, delicate children wrapped in linen swaddling
> cloths? *The Attribute of Justice replied and said,* "Is it right to kill priest and
> prophet in the temple of the LORD, *as you killed Zechariah son of Iddo the High
> Priest, a faithful prophet, in the Temple of the LORD on the Day of Atonement, because he re-
> proached you, that you should not do wrong before the LORD?"*

The first thing to notice is that the targum—apparently taking the
reference to cannibalism literally rather than as the literary trope that
it most likely is—makes it clear that the daughters of Israel ate their
children "from starvation," thereby deflecting some of the blame
(however slightly).[36] But more importantly, the targum reads this
verse as though it were a dialogue, with the second half of the verse
placed in the mouth of the divine Attribute of Justice (מדת דינא).[37]
The importance of this is twofold for my reading of Lamentations.
First, it shows that the targum, like my reading, recognized that the
focus of Zion's concern in the biblical text was the children—it is indeed these to whom YHWH has been so ruthless. The last line of the
verse, concerning priest and prophet, is effectively separated off by
attributing it to another speaker, thereby leaving the focus of the first
half of the verse solely on the children; though by this move the targum has lessened the effect of the children as summary figures for
the inhabitants of the city. Second, the targum, more explicitly than
in 1:16, senses the unfulfilled need for a response from God to the
charges of Zion. According to my reading, the rhetoric of Lamentations was geared toward eliciting a response from God, with the fate
of the children utilized here because this is what earlier achieved the
desired result from the poet. Targum Lamentations supplements the

biblical book with an answer from the divine at just this moment when the absence of God's voice is most prominent.

The answer given is, in my judgment, a non sequitur in light of the nature of Zion's appeal. The Attribute of Justice replies to the question of whether it is right for YHWH to cause the cannibalizing of children by asking a question in return and by bringing into the conversation the stoning of the prophet Zechariah (2 Chron. 24:15–22) by the people of Israel.[38] It is not even clear that the reference to Zechariah is meant to be a justification for the "punishment" now meted out on Israel. The Attribute of Justice does not say "Because of this . . ." It seems rather to be a case of competing accusations, in the form of rhetorical questions, i.e., "Who has done the worse deeds?" And if the implication of punishment is to be seen here, the Attribute of Justice's response is no response at all. Zion in Lamentations was little concerned with why the punishment was taking place, and made no claims for the sinlessness of the people. She was more concerned with the survival of the children, the barbarous treatment of whom precludes any justification or theodic settlement.

Lamentations 2:22

The next major supplement in the targum grows out of just this need in Lamentations for the issue of the children's survival to be addressed. The text of 2:22, the final verse of Zion's speech, reads:

> You called, as on a festival day,
>   attackers from all around.
> On the day of the LORD's wrath,
>   there were none who survived or escaped;
> those whom I bore and reared,
>   my enemies have consumed.

As noted above, this speech (like the book as a whole) ends on a somber and disturbing note. There are no survivors among Zion's children.

The targum to 2:22 has only one major supplement, but it is a supplement of great consequence. The targum reads:

> You will proclaim freedom to your people the house of Israel, by the hand of the messiah
> king, as you did by the hand of Moses and Aaron on the day that you brought forth Israel

from Egypt. And my youths will gather all around from *every place where they were scattered* on the day of your fierce anger, O LORD, when there was no escapee or survivor among them. Those whom I had wrapped in linen, and those whom I had nourished with *regal delicacies,* my enemies consumed.[39]

The transformation from the original text is striking. The festival day of biblical Lamentations, so bitterly ironic in its original context, is here transformed into the day of messianic redemption. And the enemies who had gathered from all around in the book of Lamentations become in the targumic version Zion's children gathering "around and around" (חזור חזור) her. Though the changes are extensive, they are not random or purposeless. Churgin holds that the midrashic element here is "obviously a sign of later addition" to the *peshat* (or literal meaning) of the original targumic text.[40] Levine argues instead that the targumist "struggled to inject a positive note," and that the reference to messianic redemption was generated by "the juxtaposition of 'the day of your wrath' and 'slaughtered' with 'as to a festival.'"[41]

I agree with Levine that one cannot so easily separate the interpretive from the literal—the *derash* from the *peshat*—in the targum, and that this particular supplement is indeed generated by the text itself. But in my judgment, it is generated not merely from a juxtaposition of images, but from the inherent (but frustrated) drive, found in Lamentations, for the survival of the children. In reference to Benjamin's essay on translation, Derrida writes:

> And if the original calls for a complement, it is because at the origin it was not there without fault, full, complete, total, identical to itself. From the origin of the original to be translated there is fall and exile.[42]

The targumist (consciously or not) apprehends this lack and supplies the midrashic complement for which "the original calls."[43] While focusing on the first half of this complement/supplement,[44] which deals with the hoped-for messianic king, Levine misses the fact that this theme is introduced as a means to imagine the survival of the children. The addition begins with the messianic hope, but leads to the climax where "my youths will gather together from every place where they were scattered on the day of your fierce anger, O LORD." The source for this phrase is likely Ezekiel 34:12, where God is portrayed as a shepherd seeking out a scattered flock: "I will rescue them

from all the places to which they were scattered on a day of cloud and
gloom" (והצלתי אתהם מכל-המקומת אשר נפצו שם ביום ענן וערפל).
If this is the case, and the nearly precise lexical equivalency suggests
that it is, then the messianic reference in the targum may be tied to
this citation of Ezekiel 34. For later in the chapter Yhwh promises to
appoint "a single shepherd to tend them: my servant David"
(34:23). The promised restoration of a Davidic king in Ezekiel 34 is
carried over into the targum as the hope for a messianic king. The
targum's move to imagine the children restored is all the more bold
in its placement alongside the original statement that "there was no
escapee or survivor among them." How can children return when
there was no survivor in the first place? The targum is not bothered
by the logical inconsistency. (Indeed, there is a sense in which—
since it is the very lack articulated by the original statement that generates the supplemental counterstatement—the former must be preserved to justify the existence of the latter.) Survival for the targum
is imagined "as if we had a future"; sur-vival is "to live again."[45]

While the targum, on this reading, is concerned to complete the
lack (what Derrida appropriately calls "the fall and exile") of the
original, it too is frustrated. This is most obvious, I think, in the clash
between what is said by the Attribute of Justice in verse 20 and what
is said by Zion in verse 22. Consider now the complete passage of
2:20–22 in Targum Lamentations:

> Look O Lord and pay attention from heaven: Whom have you af-
> flicted like these? Is it right that from starvation the daughters of Israel
> should eat the fruit of their wombs, delicate children wrapped in linen
> swaddling cloths? The Attribute of Justice replied and said, "Is it right to
> kill priest and prophet in the Temple of the Lord, as you killed Zechariah
> son of Iddo the High Priest, a faithful prophet, in the Temple of the Lord
> on the day of Atonement, because he reproached you, that you should
> not do wrong before the Lord?"
>
> The young and the old, who used to lie on silken pillows and ivory
> couches, slept in the dirt of the streets. My girls and boys have fallen, slain
> by the sword. You have slain in the day of your wrath. You have slaugh-
> tered and did not pity.
>
> You will proclaim freedom to your people the house of Israel, by the
> hand of the Messiah king, as you did by the hand of Moses and Aaron on
> the day that you brought forth Israel from Egypt. And my youths will

gather all around from every place where they were scattered on the day
of your fierce anger, O Lord, when there was no escapee or survivor
among them. Those whom I had wrapped in linen, and those whom I
had nourished with regal delicacies, my enemies consumed.

Both speaking voices address a lacuna in the original: the Attribute
of Justice tries to provide the divine response that was missing in the
original, and Zion imagines the return of her children that was
unimaginable in the original. While attempting to fill the same lack
in Lamentations that produced the response in Second Isaiah, the
targum does so in a strikingly different way. In the targum the positive element, the messianic restoration of children, is spoken only by
the voice of Zion. This is what Zion *wants* to hear from YHWH, and
it is basically what the Zion figure in Second Isaiah *does* hear.[46] But
unlike the rhetorical project of Second Isaiah, the concern of Targum Lamentations does not seem quite so focused on "comfort."
The voice of the divine in the targum is more harshly critical than the
voice of the divine in Second Isaiah. But this contrast in the divine
voice between the two "survivals" of Lamentations points also to an
interesting contrast in the respective voices of the Zion figures. As I
noted in the previous chapter, in Second Isaiah the voice of Zion is
largely eliminated by God's extended responses to her. She has become, unlike the persona of Zion in biblical Lamentations, a passive
figure. However, the divine refusal to comfort in Targum Lamentations seems to allow room for a revitalized Zion figure. Thus one
finds here again a bolder, more impassioned Zion than in Second
Isaiah, one who states right back to the divine that "you will proclaim freedom to your people . . ." Though not explicitly identified
as a request, it is possible to read this statement in Targum Lamentations 2:22 in such a way. It is also possible, however, to read it as an
imperative to God. In either case, Zion takes it upon herself to give
voice to the restoration that God has avoided speaking of, and by
doing so refuses the divine Attribute of Justice the last word.

Though both voices in the targum text of 2:20–22 are produced
by a lacuna in the original, the gap between them produces another
lacuna, or at least a conflict of interpretation. The voice correspon-
ding to Zion in the Masoretic text continues her emphasis on survival
and accusation of God and deemphasizes notions of sin and punish-

ment; but the Attribute of Justice presents just the opposite perspective. Thus one finds a text in conflict with itself, a situation not unlike the book of Lamentations itself. If one follows Benjamin's notions of translation, this is to be expected: "both the original and the translation [are] recognizable as fragments of a greater language."[47] But this greater language, or "pure" language, "does not exist, except as a permanent disjunction which inhibits all languages as such."[48] Fragments engender their survival in other fragments, whose existence is just as incomplete and precarious. The survival of literature is not a clean, decisive process, but is rather a complex process of growth and mutation. The result is not a finished product, but a stage in the afterlife of literature.

The Terms of Survival in Targum Lamentations

It is clear that Targum Lamentations, like Second Isaiah, is significantly aware of the challenges voiced by Zion in Lamentations 1 and 2, and it attempts to address them in a manner similar to Second Isaiah. However, as I hinted in the introduction to this chapter, there are significant differences in these two "survivals" of Lamentations. While Second Isaiah is looking buoyantly forward to the restoration of Jerusalem and the return of the exiles, the targum comes in the aftermath of the destruction of the second temple. As the decades of the Babylonian exile (the context of Second Isaiah) turn into the centuries of the diaspora (the context of the targum), the rhetoric of survival must take on new forms to meet this new sociohistorical context. So it is no surprise that, while the supplement to 2:22 valiantly imagines the return of Zion's children, it can do so only in a postponed messianic era. The buoyancy of the expected restoration in Second Isaiah is replaced in the targum by the need for "constituting a nation-in-exile."[49]

It is noteworthy that in articulating this project the targum has focused its interpretive energies most intensely on chapters 1 and 2. The reason for this, in my judgment, is that chapters 1 and 2 are the locus of the theological "action" in Lamentations. These chapters mount the most sustained challenge both to YHWH and to the reader, and these chapters are more insistent than the rest in their demand for an answer. As is clear from the review of scholarship in the introduction, this judgment about the importance of chapters 1 and 2

flies in the face of much twentieth-century scholarly work on the
book, which has tended to find its critical purchase in the male figure of Lamentations 3. Levine follows this line of thinking in his
analysis of the theological bent of the targum, which he deems to be
the locus classicus in targumic literature for any theology of exile.
Levine focuses on one of the few interpretive expansions outside
chapters 1 and 2 of the targum—the gloss on 3:27–28, which reads:

> It is good for a man while young to train himself to bear the yoke of the
> commandments. Let him sit alone and keep silent, bearing the sufferings
> that come upon him for the sake of the unity of the name of God, these
> being sent to punish him for the minor infractions that he commits in
> this world, until He have mercy upon him and remove them from him.
> He may accept him purified in the world-to-come.[50]

Levine argues that here we find the "theological self-definition of Israel in exile." Not surprisingly, given his decision to focus on this
particular gloss, he deems this theological self-definition to be that
of a "suffering servant accepting the yoke of God's commandments
and the suffering borne for the sake of declaring God's unity."[51] Neither should it be surprising, in light of my focus on the figure of Zion
in chapters 1 and 2 of Lamentations and Targum Lamentations, that
I find Levine's statement reductionistic. Given the extent to which
Targum Lamentations itself focuses on chapters 1 and 2, it is certainly necessary to include these chapters in any articulation of the
theological self-definition of Israel in exile. And the figure that
stands out in this case is, of course, personified Zion.

Having said this, one must ask what difference it would make to
include Zion, along with the suffering man of chapter 3, as a model
for response to exile. Most significant is the resultant challenge to the
notion of quiet acquiescence to suffering. In place of a "suffering
servant accepting the yoke" placed on him by God, this model val-
orizes the bold challenges of Mother Zion on behalf of her children.
That is, this model articulates a resistance to both the fact of exile and
the theological justification of exile. This is not to claim that the targum presents a radical subversion of the ubiquitous rabbinic concept
of the deservedness of punishment;[52] but it is to claim that Shinan's
judgment—concerning the larger nature of the targum as institution—that "the doctrine of retribution is grasped and espoused in its

most simplistic form, without the least reservation or questioning"[53] is fundamentally inadequate as a characterization of Targum Lamentations. One may admit that the targum is in fact reluctant to pursue the more radical imprecatory rhetoric of Zion in the Masoretic text of Lamentations without having to say that it is "direct, simple, manifestly didactic, and free of doubts and qualifications."[54] The targum is instead quite subtle and discerning in its recognition—and exposition—of the drive for survival in the biblical book of Lamentations. Generalized characterizations of a monolithic rabbinic doctrine of suffering or exile are inadequate. Rabbinic texts, like nearly all texts I would argue, are sites of ideological conflict, wherein the attentive reader may legitimately tease out readings counter to the generalized characterizations. This ideological (and theological) conflict will be even clearer in the following chapter on the midrash to Lamentations.

FIVE

Life in Excess:
The Midrash on Lamentations

> For any text to remain alive requires the attention and supplementation of commentary.
>
> Geoffrey Hartman

> Interpretation becomes an act of survival, and interpretation of the sacred texts ensures their survival and our own.
>
> Robert Detweiler

The two epigraphs for this chapter claim much, both about the survival of texts and about the survival of communities. Geoffrey Hartman makes his claim about how texts "remain alive" in an essay specifically devoted to the workings of midrash. The proper task of midrashic interpretation, for Hartman, is to "keep the Bible from becoming literature."[1] The survival of literature depends, paradoxically, on its *never quite becoming* literature, which would mean that a "once-living" entity had become a closed corpus. Midrash, by virtue of its unwavering attention to and vigorous supplementing of the biblical text, precludes the corpus from becoming a corpse. The rabbis understood very well this task of interpretation. Aware that Scripture had become "a closed literary corpus," the rabbis labored to reopen it by means of interpretation.

> Thus, the entirety of Scripture was spread out before the sages as the exoteric content which could be verbally recombined, analogically juxtaposed, or even harmoniously synthesized in myriad ways to make the old written Torah a "living Torah" again.[2]

The living Torah owed its life—better, its survival or afterlife—to interpretation.

Robert Detweiler's more drastic claim, that "our" survival depends on the interpretation of sacred texts, is made in relation to poststructuralist hermeneutics rather than rabbinic, but the statement holds much truth for the self-perception of rabbinic interpreters. The importance of Torah for rabbinic thought, in relation both to the world and to Israel, can hardly be overemphasized. *Pirkei Avot* (1:2) says in the name of Simon the Just, identified as one of the last survivors of the Great Assembly, that the world endures because of the study of Torah, the worship of God, and the practice of good deeds. The Talmud (b. *Pesachim* 68b) states more succinctly that were it not for Torah, heaven and earth could not endure. No less does the survival of Israel as a people depend on the Torah. A midrash on the book of Leviticus (*Sifra* 26:4) holds that had the Torah not been left with Israel when everything else was taken away, they would have been no different from the nations of the world. The survival of Israel, no less than the world, depends on the survival of the sacred texts, which in turn depend on interpretation: "When the Holy One, blessed be he, gave the Torah to Israel, he gave it only in the form of wheat, for us to make flour from it, and flax, to make a garment from it" (*Seder Eliyahu Zuta*, chap. 2).

Midrash as a Vehicle of Survival

The confessional claims of the rabbis concerning the importance of Torah and its interpretation for the survival of Judaism are not far removed from the historical claims of modern scholars. Thus, Abraham Halkin is able to write: "It is virtually a truism that religion was the chief factor for the survival of the Jews and the maintenance of their identity."[3] With the end of a Jewish political state in the second century of the Common Era and the centuries of diaspora existence that followed, the normal course of absorption and assimilation would be expected, especially for a group that invariably adopted the vernacular and many of the manners of the majority population in which they found themselves, as Jews did. While Halkin cites the "religion" of the Jews as the key factor that prevented assimilation and thus procured survival, it is necessary to be more specific; for it is not just religion in general that galvanized Judaism in the beginning centuries of the Common Era, but *a certain kind* of religion. Concomitant with the change in political fortunes of Jewry came a drastic change in the religion itself, so that the religion that was so important in the survival of diaspora Jewry was itself a "survival"— in Benjamin's sense of both transformation and renewal—of earlier forms of Judaism.

The most significant change in the religion of Judaism at this time was of course the shift from a priest-centered cultus to a rabbi-centered textuality. While the destruction of the Jerusalem temple in 70 C.E. is often cited as the key turning point in this shift, the long-term significance of the destruction of the temple, and the need to re-create a Judaism capable of procuring the survival of the *people* Israel in place of the *nation* Israel, was not fully realized until the second century C.E.. For example, it has been argued that the uprisings among Jews in Egypt, North Africa, and Cyprus in 115–17 C.E. were occasioned by the failure of Trajan to authorize the rebuilding of the temple. And the Bar Kochba rebellion of 132–35 C.E. was fueled by the hope of restoration of Jewish independence and the temple service.[4] Only after this failed rebellion was Jerusalem finally forbidden to Jews and the land of Israel renamed Syria Palaestina. In the years following the defeat of Bar Kochba it became clear once and for all that the religion of the second temple would not be able to survive unchanged; neither could it serve as the basis for the survival of diaspora Judaism.

Although the temple cultus could no longer serve as the center of Jewish religion, the Bible could. While it is a mistake to see all rabbinic activity and literature as exegesis, it is true that the biblical text became a sort of portable homeland that was able to unite Jews who had no physical homeland. And rabbinic interpretation, both halakhic and aggadic, became the primary way that the text was kept alive. As James Kugel writes, "[W]hat the Rabbis had founded was a religion of interpretation, a tradition of studying Scripture and putting it into practice that touched every member of the community."[5] Interpretation of the sacred texts took on such importance that even God was portrayed in a midrash as a scholar poring over God's own Torah (*b. Berakhot* 8b).

This religion of interpretation produced interpretation in excess.

M. M. Kasher's monumental collection of midrash devotes fifty-two pages to rabbinic interpretation of Genesis 1:1.[6] The midrash to Lamentations contains no fewer than fourteen proems (introductory comments, called in Hebrew *petihtaot*) devoted to the phrase "How solitary sits the city" and thirteen devoted simply to the single word "alas" (איכה). To use Robert Detweiler's characterization of interpretation in general, midrashic interpretation is a process of "piling on,"[7] that is, piling more texts onto the Bible. Midrash is by nature "excessive": it produces more textuality than would seem to be warranted. Thus, midrash will fill in dialogue between characters that the Bible leaves unreported. It will provide motivations for the actions of characters that the Bible leaves unmotivated. It will seemingly produce out of thin air elaborate detail and ingenious stories as it goes about its work of interpretation. Like targum, midrash has no desire to replace or bury the biblical text, but is in fact concerned with its survival. To return to Hartman's characterization of interpretation, it is just this "attention" and "supplementation" that procure the biblical text's survival. Unlike targum, the attention and supplementation of midrash is not constrained to reading between the lines of Scripture. While targum must faithfully reproduce the biblical text to which it is attending and work its supplements into the text, midrash may construct extended narratives of interpretation that, though often having the biblical text as its warp and woof, are not required to reproduce the text in toto.

Attention and supplementation are certainly qualities well represented in midrash; but there are those who would doubt its status as commentary, arguing that midrashic interpretation is driven by something other than an exegetical impulse. Maimonides, in his *Guide of the Perplexed* for example, describes midrashim (the plural of midrash) as having the "status of poetical conceits; they are not meant to bring out the meaning of the text in question."[8] Modern scholars, until recently, have tended to follow suit in seeing midrashic activity as only loosely connected with the biblical text it purports to interpret. The influential scholar of rabbinics Max Kadushin summarizes what has traditionally been the critical position when he writes that "a haggadic interpretation is not logically related to the text which it interprets: the text has been a non-determining stimulus."[9] Now, however, scholars are beginning explore midrash

as exegesis of the biblical text.[10] Often this takes the form of an explanation of midrash as concerned to "fill the gaps" in Biblical law and
narrative.[11] But this understanding hardly accounts for the seeming
joy that midrash takes in providing numerous ways of filling any one
gap, signified by the frequent midrashic phrase, "Another interpretation . . ." (דבר אחר). I prefer to imagine midrash as attending to
the gaps in Scripture, but instead of filling them, widening them.
Midrash opens the biblical text out to the vast multiplicity of (often
conflicting) interpretive avenues available; yet it never abandons the
text on which these multiple interpretations are based. In this chapter I will pursue how the quite looming "gap" left by the absence of
God's voice in the book of Lamentations is subject to this interpretive excess in the major collection of midrashim on Lamentations
(known as Eikhah Rabbah), and in particular how the problems
raised by the absence of God's voice are tied to the deaths of Zion's
children.

The Persuasion of God and the Survival
of Children in Eikhah Rabbah

One can identify a number of places in Eikhah Rabbah where the
theme of the suffering of children is a point of interpretive expansion. Here, however, I want to focus on a particularly striking text
found in the twenty-fourth *petihta* of Eikhah Rabbah. There have been
three very astute treatments of this narrative in recent years,[12] but it
warrants closer attention in light of my reading of Lamentations and
its demand for an answer from God on behalf of Zion's children. I
will argue that the two major drives of the narrative in Eikhah Rabbah—the weeping and mourning of God and a concern for abused
children—derive from the fundamental (but unmet) drive for survival found in the book of Lamentations.

The narrative comes at the end of the *petihta* and offers a third interpretation of Isaiah 22:12, "And in that day did the LORD, the God
of hosts, call to weeping, and to lamentation, and to baldness, and
to girding with sackcloth."[13] Interpreters are agreed that the narrative has undergone extensive redactional activity, and there are undoubtedly at least two discrete stories (and quite possibly three) that
have been combined. David Stern has noted that "each of the narratives represents God as having a personality so unlike the other that

they are virtual opposites," and he has argued that what connects the separate portrayals is the fact that "they share a common subject, God's behavior in the aftermath of the Destruction of the Second Temple."[14] This does not explain, though, why the many other narratives that also share this subject were not conflated in a similar way. While it is possible that no more than the accidents of textual transmission are responsible for the final form of our text, I will argue that there is a more explicit rhetorical-theological function at work.

God's Response and the Loss of Children

The first of the two stories that make up the larger narrative is the shorter and is presented as an anonymous interpretation (that is, not attributed to a particular rabbi) of Isaiah 22:12. It opens with an account of a dilemma faced by God when "the Holy One, blessed be He, decided to destroy the temple." The problem is that as long as God is dwelling in the temple the nations are unable to destroy it; therefore God resolves to withdraw from it "until the end" (i.e., the coming of the Messiah). The enemy immediately burns the temple, and God follows through by withdrawing the Shekhinah (the aspect of the divine that is present on earth) to its "former place," the proof text of which action is given as Hosea 5:15, "I will go and return to my place, until they realize their guilt and seek my face." After the withdrawal of the Shekhinah and subsequent destruction of the temple, God undergoes a remarkable emotional transformation:

> At that moment the Holy One, blessed be He, wept and said, "Alas! What have I done? I brought my Shekhinah to rest on earth because of Israel, but now that they have sinned I have returned to my former place. Heaven forbid that I should become a laughingstock to the nations and a mockery to humankind." At that moment Metatron came in and fell upon his face and said to him, "Master of the Universe, I shall weep, but you cannot weep!" He replied, "If you will not let me weep now, I will take myself to a place where you are not permitted to follow, and there I will weep, as it is stated: 'For if you will not listen, my soul shall weep in secret for pride.'" (Jer. 13:17)

In his study of the anthropomorphic nature of this *petihta*, Stern has pointed out that from the moment God leaves the temple, God is "hopelessly entrapped in the pathos of human existence," and that from this point on the narrative charts God's "descent into the depths of mourning."[15] At this early stage, God is primarily lamenting over God's own abject state. That is, God seems most concerned with the loss of a dwelling place and how the nations might jeer at what would seem to be a failure of God's. There is as yet very little concern for the human victims of the destruction, since God, by using the phrase "but now that they have sinned," squarely places the blame for God's lamentable state on the shoulders of the Jewish victims. But it will become clear below that God's journey into mourning has only begun.

After refusing consolation from Metatron, God resolves to see firsthand (along with the attending angels, and led by Jeremiah) the extent of the destruction caused by the enemy.[16] The sight moves God again to tears:

> At that moment the Holy One, blessed be He, wept and said, "I am in anguish because of my house. My children, where are you? My priests, where are you? My loved ones, where are you? What shall I do for you? I warned you, but you did not turn back in repentance."

God then turns to Jeremiah and compares the divine person to a man who builds a marriage canopy for his son, only to have the son die under it. God asks of Jeremiah: "Do you not feel pain? Not for me? Not for my children? Go and summon Abraham, Isaac, and Jacob, and Moses from their sepulchers, for they know how to weep." Stern argues that God continues here to "bewail His losses, His helplessness, His failure to prevent the Destruction," and that God becomes both victim and mourner, effectively shutting out the human victims of the destruction.[17] But I would maintain that there is in fact a genuine opening out of divine concern here for the human victims: God laments not just God's own state, but, as is made clear in the accusation to Jeremiah, God's "children" as well. To be sure, God is still the subject of the narrative, and it is God's grief at the loss of children that is most acute; but the language has shifted from "Israel," who were portrayed as sinners in the opening section, to God's "children," who are here portrayed as victims. There is still a hint of reproach in God's lament—"seeing that I warned you but you did not repent"—but even this will be gone by the end of the *petihta*.

Following God's instructions, Jeremiah summons the patriarchs, although he balks at telling them what happened to "our children," claiming ignorance of the reason behind the summons. He rouses Moses as well, who is able to find out about the destruction from "the ministering angels, whom he recognized from the time of the giving of the Torah." Moses cries and wails until he reaches the patriarchs, who also cry and wail at the news, and together all four move on to meet God at the gates of the temple. The final climactic scene of the first half of the narrative is focused around the key verse of Isaiah 22:12.

> As soon as the Holy One, blessed be He, saw them, immediately "[i]n that day the LORD, the God of hosts, called for weeping and for lamenting, for tonsuring and for girding with sackcloth" (Isa. 22:12). Were it not stated in Scripture it would not be possible to say such a thing, but they went weeping from gate to gate like a man whose dead is lying before him, and the Holy One, blessed be He, lamented and said, "Woe to the king who prospers in his youth but fails in his old age!"

The audacity of the midrash is amply displayed with this passage, as God joins the patriarchs in an uncontrollable weeping and alludes to divine failure. God's descent into mourning has gone to the extreme. Drawing on talmudic discussions of the disruptive nature of grief (*Berakhot* 3:1), Stern argues that God is here portrayed as an "*onein.*"

> According to the halakhah, *aninut*, the state of being an *onein*, is the most terrible grief a person can suffer; the *onein* is considered to be so bereft, so shaken by his loss that he is not required to pray or to observe the positive commandments of the Law. [18]

The story ends then with God having reached the most abject state possible, both emotionally and halakhically. The divine subjectivity is shattered; God can only mourn the loss of God's "child" and admit failure on the part of the divine.

It may be worthwhile at this point to see where the narrative stands in relation to my reading of Lamentations 1 and 2. The midrashic text under consideration has picked up the two major themes that I identified in the biblical book of Lamentations: (1) the attempt to elicit a response from God; and (2) the concern for threatened children. With regard to the first theme, one could hardly witness more of a response from God than that portrayed by the midrash:

God has taken up the posture of personified Zion in Lamentations, that of mourner. One may recall that this is the response of the poet to Zion and presumably what the poet hoped would happen when he encouraged Zion to continue to cry out to Yhwh (Lam. 2:18–19). With regard to the second theme, it is of course the loss of children (or a child) that has engendered the response and brought God to the state of emotional breakdown and halakhic liminality. While the depth of God's grief in this story is unmatched elsewhere in Eikhah Rabbah, there are other places where God is portrayed as weeping over the destruction. Shaye Cohen writes that this collection of dirges and laments "becomes a source of consolation since it is God himself who is reciting the dirges and the laments."[19] This is true as far as it goes, but like Second Isaiah and Targum Lamentations, the midrash discerns a need to go beyond just engaging God's grief and imagines a restoration of the lost children. That is, to return to our governing metaphor, the midrash reads for survival. The radical hermeneutical power of the midrashic imagination is not content simply with consolation for life lost; it moves further in imagining life restored—the "more life" preserved in the French word survie. And so, whatever the redactional history of this petihta might be, the text as we have it now pushes on, determined that Zion's children will live again. Or, to put it in the terms of the literature of survival that I reviewed in chapter one, the desire for persuasion has been fulfilled: the lament of the patriarchs has become God's lament.

God's Response and the Return of Children

The second portion of the narrative from petihta 24 is the longer and is presented as an interpretation of Rabbi Samuel bar Nahman.[20] The difference in the character of God as portrayed in this section in comparison with that of the previous section is striking. God "is removed, utterly distant from the narrative's human characters in a way He never is in the first narrative."[21] Unlike in the previous narrative, God is largely absent as a speaking subject here. When God does speak, it is virtually always (excepting the climactic last paragraph) in the role of accuser or judge of Israel. Throughout the story, the patriarchs and Moses—in roles parallel to that of personified Zion in Lamentations—repeatedly defend Israel and attempt to provoke an emotional response in God by bringing the suffering caused by the destruction to God's attention. But most strikingly for my reading, it is "Rachel, our mother" (רחל אמנו) who in the end has the desired effect on God.

This portion of our text opens with Abraham weeping and lamenting bitterly before God. He asks God for an explanation for the shame and contempt heaped upon Israel, but receives no answer. The attending angels, however, are apparently moved by Abraham, and they join in the lamenting themselves.

> As soon as the ministering angels saw him, they also began to string together line after line of lament, saying "The streets are desolate, the travelers have disappeared, etc." (Isa. 33:8). What is the meaning of "The streets are desolate?": The ministering angels said to the Holy One, blessed be he, "The streets that you laid straight to Jerusalem, so that the stream of travelers would never be broken—How they have become desolate!" What is the meaning of "The travelers have disappeared?": The ministering angels said to the Holy One, blessed be he, "Israel used to fill the streets coming and going to the festivals—How they have disappeared!"

Taking sides with Abraham and against God, the angels use the passage's proof text of Isaiah 33:8 as an occasion to accuse God of neglecting Israel. The verse from Isaiah employed by the midrash here, it should be noted, is essentially a paraphrase of the opening verses of the book of Lamentations, where one reads that "Zion's roads are in mourning, empty of festival pilgrims" (1:4). This allusion is made more explicit by the angels' twofold use of "How" (היאך) to open their laments, thus alluding to the opening "Alas/How" (איכה) of the book of Lamentations. The angels continue to explicate the proof text from Isaiah, claiming no less than that God has broken the covenant with Abraham. In the speech of the angels, Isaiah 33:8c, "he has rejected (מאס) the cities," becomes a cipher for "You have rejected (מאסת) Jerusalem and Zion after you have chosen them." This is in turn connected with a verse from Jeremiah, "Have you utterly rejected (המאס מאסת) Judah? Has your soul loathed Zion?" (14:19).

In this short but densely woven intertextual nexus, the midrash spans the length of the book of Lamentations and concisely restates its

central themes. As the beginning of the angels' speech paraphrases
the opening of Lamentations, so the end of their speech paraphrases
the final unanswered appeal of Lamentations 5. For can one fail to
read the quote from Jeremiah 14:19 in light of Lamentations 5:22,
"Have you utterly rejected us (כי אם מאס מאסתנו)? Are you exceedingly angry with us?"[22] Faithful to the creative spirit of the petihta
genre, the midrash disdains simply to cite the verses from Lamentations. Instead, it prefers to work out its exegetical program with reference to other biblical texts. The petihta demonstrates here what Stern
has called the "fundamental tendency of midrash, the urge to unite
the diverse parts of scripture into a single and seamless whole re-
flecting the unity of God's will."[23] I would want to nuance this statement, particularly in light of the text under consideration, so that it is
less focused on the "unity" of God's will in favor of the plurality that
is sponsored by the midrashic imagination. Nevertheless, Stern's
main point about the freedom of midrash to bring to bear seemingly
unrelated portions of Scripture on its exegetical program is certainly
demonstrated here. What is also demonstrated is that these verses are
not imported simply to show the interpreter's ingenuity or knowledge of Scripture, but serve as exegetical comments on the text at hand
(in this case Lamentations). Thus, both within the "infrastructure" of
the petihta (the specific interpretations of proof texts such as we have
here) and within the "superstructure" of the petihta (the larger movement served by these local interpretive comments) we find an adher-
ence to the biblical text under consideration.[24] The extent to which
this is true for the superstructure will become clearer below.

The angels manage to provoke a response from God, but the response is manifestly not acceptable to the midrash. God's initial entry into this portion of the narrative comes as a question that shows
a lack of comprehension: "Why do you string dirges together over
this incident, standing rows upon rows?" Expressing their solidarity
with Abraham, the angels cite God's failure to respond to Abraham's
lamenting. God responds in turn with a midrash of God's own,
"Since the day that my beloved died and went to his eternal home,
he has not come into my house—and now 'What is my beloved [i.e.,
Abraham] doing in my house?'" (Jer. 11:15). Although refusing still
to be moved by the angels' laments, it must be noted that when God
quotes Jeremiah 11:15 the context is changed from one of judgment

(as the verse functions in Jeremiah) to one of personal affront: God's feelings are hurt from lack of attention. The way is open for Abraham to press the issue:

> Abraham said to the Holy One, blessed be He, "Lord of the World, why have you exiled my children and delivered them into the hands of the gentiles who have ruthlessly murdered them, and why have you destroyed the temple, the place where I sacrificed my son Isaac as a burnt offering before you?"

The question is packed with allusions. It reflects the persistent midrashic legend that Abraham in fact carried out the sacrifice of Isaac, rather than being stopped by the angel of the LORD as Genesis 22 states.[25] Mobilizing this theme here, I think, serves to contrast *Abraham's faithfulness* in carrying out God's irrational will with *God's unfaithfulness* to Israel. It also, perhaps, indicts God for failing to stay the hand of Abraham at the last moment (as happens in the biblical account). Isaac, of course, becomes a symbol for Abraham's other "children" (i.e., his descendants) who suffer death and abuse at the destruction of Jerusalem.

God answers (no doubt attempting to settle the issue) that "your children sinned, transgressing the whole of the Torah and the twenty-two letters in which it is composed." God offers another proof text, "All Israel has transgressed your Torah" (Dan. 9:11), in the service of this allusion to the acrostic structure of the poems of Lamentations.[26] God's answer—that punishment is due to sin—is a common one in rabbinic literature and one might expect it to serve as the final word on the matter. But that is not the case, as Abraham demands, and receives, a trial of sorts. God calls witnesses against Israel, and Abraham refutes them. In a wonderful scene, Abraham dissuades first the Torah and then each successive letter of the alphabet from testifying against Israel, to whom he refers five times as "my children."

From this point to the end of the *petihta*, God's voice is even more absent from the narrative. After refuting the called witnesses, Abraham presses his case on behalf of Israel further, joined by Isaac, Jacob, and finally Moses. Interpreters have characterized the appeals of the patriarchs as based upon their "great deeds"[27] or "individual merits."[28] While this is no doubt one aspect of their argument, what stands out in particular is the emphasis on those merits relating to

the children of the patriarchs. Abraham reminds God of his pain when
God demanded the sacrifice of Isaac, made more poignant by the
emphasis on Abraham's age and the unexpected blessing of Isaac.
"Will you not remember this on my behalf, and will you not have
mercy on my children?" Abraham asks. Isaac himself speaks up and
takes the role of threatened child. "Will you not remember this on
my behalf, and will you not have mercy on my children?" Isaac asks.
Jacob relates how Esau "sought to kill my children, and I risked my
life on their behalf." Jacob admits the "pain of child rearing" and the
trouble he experienced on account of his children, but that it is no
excuse for abandoning them. (The implications for God are clear.)
"Will you not remember this on my behalf to have mercy on my
children?" asks Jacob in his turn.

Coming on the heels of these closely paralleled rhetorical patterns, the speech of Moses that follows seems a non sequitur. But in-
terpreting it in terms of the rhetorical flow of the passage as a whole,
we find some light shed on its function here. Moses appeals not to
his role in a parent-child relationship as the patriarchs do, but rather
to his role as "a faithful shepherd to Israel." But it is clear in the context of the pattern established by the patriarchs that Israel is represented as the "children" of Moses, perhaps an allusion to Numbers
11, where Moses contends with God over which of them has the responsibility to care for Israel. This identification of Israel as children
serves to remind that "children" throughout this study represent Israel in relation to God. That is not to say that the lived suffering of
"real" children is of no account to our texts; but rather that this physical suffering was deemed as the appropriate metaphorical vehicle
for the tenor of Israel. With Moses' speech this metaphorical identification is made explicit for definite rhetorical purposes. That is,
Moses makes clear to God that Israel are God's children and that God
should be at least as concerned with them as the patriarchs were with
their children. This is the meaning of Moses' complaint that he took
care of Israel during the bad times in the desert and now that they
are exiled; while God took over only during the good times represented by the entry to the promised land. God is willing neither to
bear the pain of child rearing (to use Jacob's words) nor the task of
lamenting. In short, God has shirked God's duties as parent to God's
children, Israel.

God remains silent before the accusations of Moses and the patriarchs, which fact apparently resolves Moses to attempt to redeem the Israelites on his own. Perhaps imagining a second exodus, Moses recruits Jeremiah to go with him to Babylon "to bring them in." The exiles see Moses and exclaim, "the son of Amram has come from his grave to liberate us from the hands of our enemies." It is only at this point that a semblance of divine response is interjected, and only as a *bat kol* (a voice from heaven) proclaiming that "this is a decree from me": the exile will continue. When Moses returns to the patriarchs with his report, there is an intensification of rhetoric.

> As soon as Moses reached the patriarchs of the world, they asked him, "What have our enemies done to our children?" He replied, "Some of them were killed, some had their hands bound behind their backs, some were bound in iron chains, some were stripped naked, some died in the road and were left for the birds of the air and the beasts of the earth, and some lay exposed to the sun, hungry and thirsty."
>
> Immediately, they all began to weep and to sing dirges: "Woe! What has happened to our children? How you have become like orphans without a father! How you have had to sleep in the hot summer sun with no clothes or coverings! How you have walked over rocks and stones, stripped of shoes and without sandals! How you were loaded with heavy sacks of sand! How your hands were bound behind you! How you could not even swallow the spit in your mouths!"

The story has focused in even closer on the suffering of the children, which is here elaborated upon with concrete images of abuse and neglect. With God cast as the role of absent parent, the theological audacity of the midrash is astounding.

This point in the narrative represents what was apparently a final story in one version of the *petihta*.[29] This story has Moses (not God, one notes) charging the captors of the Jews "not [to] kill with a cruel death" by killing a child in the presence of the parent. But in fact the Babylonians do not only that, but even worse, by making a father slay his own son in the presence of the child's mother. This version of the narrative ends with the mother weeping, her tears falling on the body of the child. But the *petihta* cannot end this way; the drive for survival is too strong. As the text of Lamentations generated texts that survive it, so does the earlier version of the *petihta* require something more. So the midrash makes a final assault on God's sensibilities in hopes of garnering the desired response. Most strikingly, it does so by mobilizing the person of "Rachel, our mother" (רחל אמנו). This supplement to the *petihta* begins with Moses citing the Torah against God: that is, he uses the requirement of Leviticus 22:28 that a mother animal and its young not be sacrificed on the same day to indict God. "Have they not killed many, many mothers and sons," he laments, "and you are silent!" The importance of Rachel entering the narrative at just this point can hardly be overstated. In the same way that the violent description of the deaths of her children prompted Mother Zion to interrupt the poet of Lamentations to accuse God, so here does the rhetoric of the *petihta* prompt Mother Rachel to do likewise. As Neusner's translation puts it: "Then Rachel, our mother, leapt into the fray."[30] Thus the weeping mother with whom the earlier version ended is transformed into the matriarch Rachel, a figure both more concrete and more archetypal in nature.

As with the patriarchs immediately preceding in the narrative, it is easy to construe Rachel's speech as merely a recitation of her past deeds. Thus, for example, both Stern and Kraemer present God as yielding to Rachel's "argument" that "as she had overcome her jealousy of her sister Leah . . . , so should God overcome God's jealousy of the idols—who are nothing, after all—and have compassion on Israel."[31] Or as Stern writes, "How can such petty jealousy on His part justify Israel's great shame and national disgrace?"[32] But as with the patriarch's arguments with God, this reading—though once again true as far as it goes—overlooks what I take to be the most important aspect of Rachel's presence in the narrative. This is, of course, Rachel's embodiment of concern over the fate of children. It is true that Rachel's speech is on the whole about her willingness to comply with Laban's plot to have Leah marry Jacob, and she does indeed use this to expose the pettiness of God's actions with regard to Israel. On this much I am in agreement with Stern and Kraemer. But one cannot overlook the climactic final line of Rachel's appeal, which emphasizes the result of God's pettiness:

> Why should you, everlasting and merciful King, be jealous of idolatry in which there is no reality? Why should you exile my children, let them be murdered by the sword, and permit the enemy to do with them whatever they please?

Thus, the burden of Rachel's argument concerning her loyalty to Leah is—as we have seen again and again in the narrative in other forms—to affront God with the suffering of her children in the hope of eliciting a compassionate response. Against all theological odds, Rachel's appeal succeeds in moving God:

> Immediately, the mercy of the Holy One, blessed be He, was stirred, and He said, "For your sake, Rachel, I will restore Israel to their place." As it is written: "Thus says the LORD: A voice is heard in Ramah, lamentation and bitter wailing, Rachel wailing for her children. She refuses to be comforted for her children, because they are not" (Jer. 31:15). It is also written: "Thus says the LORD: Refrain your voice from wailing, and your eyes from tears; for your work shall be rewarded." It is also written: "There is hope for your future, declares the LORD, and your children shall return to their own land." (Jer. 31:16)

Here the petihta makes abundantly clear, by God's choice of proof texts, just what it is about Rachel's presence that causes God's mercy to finally well up: it is Rachel's advocacy for her children and her refusal to be comforted in their absence. Thus, I cannot agree with Stern in his judgment that "the sole motive for this change of heart [in God] seems to be shame at being found out to be so petty, not real concern or compassion for the Jews' plight."[33] I would agree instead with the following judgment by Alan Mintz:

> In the end it is neither Abraham nor Moses who effects this reorientation [of God's character]. In a parallel to the power of child suffering to break through to the poet of chapter 2 of Lamentations, it is a female voice, the voice of Mother Rachel.[34]

It is vitally important to note, in addition, that the midrash is not content here with just an emotional response from God—which after all was already effected in the first half of the narrative—but demands the survival of the children. In the impossible necessity for the children to "live again," Rachel's weeping for her children who "are not" is juxtaposed with God's promise that "your children shall return."

The Figures of Rachel and Mother Zion

There can be no doubt that Rachel functions in this petihta in a role strikingly similar to that of Mother Zion in Lamentations. But to what extent am I justified in claiming that this similarity is generated by an exegetical impulse? Stern, who elsewhere strongly emphasizes the exegetical nature of the *petihta* genre, feels that here this is not the case. Instead, he attributes the stories to the need of the Jewish community to deal with the tension between its feelings of extreme guilt and extreme self-pity in the aftermath of the destruction of the second temple. On my reading, of course, the *petihta* is emphatically exegetical. This is not to deny the historical Jewish community's need to deal with the feelings identified by Stern, but rather to suggest that the *way* these were dealt with was through the act of interpretation. Thus, the survival of the historical community is intimately linked to the survival of Lamentations in the text of Eikhah Rabbah.

Finally, in support of my claim for the exegetical nature of our *petihta*, I submit that it is no accident that the base verse with which it ends is taken from the book of Jeremiah. In the usual form of the *petihta* the base verse would be taken from the biblical book under consideration, in this case Lamentations. One of the primary functions of the *petihta* genre is to lead the hearer/reader from the intersecting verse to the base verse, which serves as the lectionary reading for the day. Therefore, the verses from Jeremiah here are manifestly standing in for the book of Lamentations, which comes as no surprise given the rabbinic view that Jeremiah was the author of Lamentations. The reader is expected to connect this base verse about Rachel's weeping with the book of Lamentations and, more specifically, with the beginning of the book, from which all other base verses in the *petihtaot* of Eikhah Rabbah are taken. Thus, my identification of Rachel in the midrash with Zion in Lamentations is not only warranted but practically demanded by the *petihta* itself. Emil Fackenheim observes that, "any rabbinic reference to children in exile would at once call to mind Jer. 31:15 ff.—the passage in which Rachel weeps for her exiled children and receives the promise of their return."[35] In light of this, we may see how the midrashic imagination, in focusing its exegetical impulse on the beginning of the book of Lamentations, where the fate of Mother Zion and her children is so central, would light upon the figure of Mother Rachel as a way of meeting the demand for survival found therein.

SIX

Poetics of Survival:
Eleazar ben Kallir's Medieval Kinot

> As music and splendor
> Survive not the lamp and the lute,
> The heart's echoes render
> No song when the spirit is mute—
> No song—but sad dirges . . .
>
> Percy Shelley

> . . . and what is a poet for in a destitute time?
>
> Friedrich Hölderlin

"*Wozu Dichter in dürftiger Zeit?*" asks the poet Hölderlin in his elegy "Bread and Wine." "What are poets for?" Or, one might translate, "What good are poets?" More particularly, what good are poets in a destitute time? The time evoked by Hölderlin, so Martin Heidegger informs us, refers to an era "defined by the god's failure to arrive, by the 'default of God.'"[1] When God has defaulted and humanity must make its own way through the deprivations of history, what are poets for? Shelley's answer to such a question, given in the form of a poem itself, is that while the spirit may be rendered mute poetry survives in "sad dirges." Poets are for putting the destitution into words, or perhaps it is better said that poets are for attaching words to the destitution. God may have defaulted, but perhaps language has not quite yet done the same. While God fails to arrive, poetry manages to survive.

Dirges and laments, simply by putting language to the destitution, by telling the truth about it, ensure at least that the spirit is not unequivocally mute. This is one answer to Hölderlin's question: the poet is "for" language. But this answer does not address the stronger force of the question. That is, are poets "good" for anything? Does poetry "do" anything beyond truth telling? Does poetry redress the destitution of the time? Another poet, Seamus Heaney, provides another answer: "The redressing effect of poetry comes from its being a glimpsed alternative, a revelation of potential that is denied or constantly threatened by circumstances."[2] What poets are good for in a destitute time is to take a last stand against just that destitution, to provide—even if only for the space of a poem—a glimpsed alternative to destitution. But to preserve Shelley's insight, the alternative must remain only *glimpsed*, never fully present. Only by admitting the destitution, by telling the truth about the circumstances of deprivation and threat that mute the spirit, can there be a revelation of potential beyond the dirge. This is what poets are good for. This mixture of overwhelming lament and a nearly overwhelmed hope is also an apt description of Eleazar ben Kallir's medieval poems of lament.

The Nature and Character of Medieval Hebrew Poetry

In the Middle Ages, the interpretive urge to "pile on" texts seems to have been channeled from midrashic interpretation into the writing of poetry. As the expanding corpus of midrashic commentary reached its final stages of collection and near-canonical status, the writing of Hebrew poetry, and in particular liturgical poems known as piyyutim (singular, piyyut), became the most prominent Jewish literary activity. The origins of the piyyutim are still a matter of scholarly speculation. There seem to have been anonymous payyetanim (writers of piyyutim; singular, payyetan) already in the first centuries of the common era, but the earliest known poets are Yose ben Yose, Yannai, and Eleazar ben Kallir. Dates proposed for Yose (the earliest) range from the second to the sixth centuries, and for Kallir they range from the fourth to the eighth.[3] Whatever their origins, by about 1200 or so, piyyutim were quite ubiquitous in Jewish centers around the world and some continued to be produced up into the modern period. Their use waned only in the nineteenth century under the influence of Reform Judaism and its twin concerns to shorten the liturgy and introduce the vernacular into it. During these centuries the payyetanim were amazingly prolific, producing tens of thousands of poems. Israel Davidson's *Thesaurus of Medieval Hebrew Poetry* lists thirty-six thousand entries, and it represents only a fraction of all piyyutim produced during the Middle Ages.

Like midrash, then, with its ever-expanding corpus of interpretive comments, the writing of piyyutim is a practice of "excessive" textuality. Indeed, there were many in Judaism who felt that the piyyutim, again like midrash, were excessive not just in their quantity but in their rhetorical and theological audacity as well. The poets delighted in constructing a web of biblical and midrashic allusions, presented in complex schemes of rhyme and acrostic patterns. And the piyyut often expresses "theological views which, even if they are not fully heretical, nevertheless represent a challenge to what has become normative and conventional."[4] It is little wonder then that one finds Maimonides writing against what he sees as the license "taken by poets and preachers or such as think that what they speak is poetry, so that the utterances of some of them constitute an absolute denial of faith."[5] Citing the Talmud (*Sukkah* 23; *Ta'anith* 25), Maimonides charges that one should not "go beyond that which has been inserted in the prayers and benedictions by the men of the Great Synagogue," and that whoever does so is guilty of making "vituperative utterances against what is above."[6] Likewise, Abraham Ibn Ezra indicts the poems of Kallir in particular because they are full of "exegetical and homiletical allusions" that depart from what he considers to be the *peshat* (or literal meaning) of the biblical text.[7]

Just these qualities, however—its allusive, exegetical style and its theological audacity—make the piyyut of particular interest for my study of the afterlife of Lamentations. Because the piyyutim were written specifically for festivals and special services and were to include reference both to the theme of the festival and to the lectionary reading for the day, one may expect to find among those piyyutim written for Tisha b'Av—the fast day commemorating the destruction of both the first and second Jewish temples, on which the scroll of Lamentations is read—a concern for Zion and her children. In the following section I will look at a selection of three piyyutim from the pen of Kallir (who is widely regarded at the greatest of Palestinian payyetanim)[8] with an eye to teasing out this exegetical trajectory. The

liturgical poems written for Tisha b'Av (or the Ninth of Av) are usually referred to as kinot (singular, kinah), or "laments."[9]

Zion and Her Children in the Kinot for Tisha b'Av

The piyyutim come relatively late in the afterlife of Lamentations.
Thus, the kinot for Tisha b'Av have at their disposal not only the text
of Lamentations, but the other biblical and rabbinic "survivals" with
which I dealt in previous chapters. Kallir, even more so than other
payyetanim, does not shy away from these texts, but incorporates them
into what seems at times an impossibly rich web of intertextuality. I
have chosen the following three poems not only because they are in-
dicative of Kallir's style and participate in the exegetical trajectory I
have identified, but also because each poem incorporates material
from or mirrors in some way the texts from Second Isaiah, Targum
Lamentations, and the midrash, respectively. By showing how all
three participate in the same trajectory, while doing so in varying
ways, I mean to show that there is a "definite structure" to the dynamic of survival even while allowing for different "versions of survival."[10]

"The Mother of Children"

The first of Kallir's poems to be considered—which I will call "The
Mother of Children" after its opening phrase (אם הבנים)—is a
striking attempt to provide the voice of God that is so noticeably absent in Lamentations. It does so by imagining an extended dialogue
between Zion and God.[11]

This acrostic piyyut is made up of six stanzas, with three stanzas
devoted to Zion's accusations against God and three devoted to God's
answering of these accusations, employing language and imagery
drawn from the Song of Songs. This poem might be judged as only
marginally related to the book of Lamentations, even given its provenance in the liturgy of Tisha b'Av, were it not for the important struc-
turing device with which both halves of the poem end. At the end of
each speaker's part—that is, the final line of the third and the sixth
stanzas, respectively—there occurs a quite concrete citation of the
word pair encountered near the end of Lamentations: "forget/aban-
don" (שכח and עזב). As I argued in chapter five, it was this same
word pair that was so important for the response provided in Isaiah

49 to the rhetoric of destruction in Lamentations. In the poem "The Mother of Children," the word pair takes on a similar importance, reinforced by its strategic repetition. Only by recognizing the citation of Lamentations 5:20 is one able to contextualize the poem as an attempt to fill the void that confronts the reader at the end of the biblical book. Without such a recognition, the reader may well see only general connections with the biblical book, as is the case with many of the piyyutim for Tisha b'Av.

The first stanza of the poem sets the mood for the speech of "the mother of children." Given the mobilization of Lamentations by the citation of 5:20, I regard the first stanza as a description of Zion, though it is not explicitly identified so. The mother's mourning is expressed by means of a number of alliterative and rhyming verbs. She moans, mourns in her heart, and roars out loud; she bursts out crying and speaks bitterly; she sheds tears, and is finally stunned into silence. This description leads into the woman's speech proper in stanzas two and three, which, outside of a few allusions such as tormenters rejoicing at her downfall and her description as an unclean woman (נדה), does not cite Lamentations overmuch. But the speech ends, as noted above, with the phrase, "Why has he forsaken me forever, forgotten me?" (למה לנצח עזבני שכחני). This is nearly a direct quote of Lamentations 5:20, "Why have you forgotten us forever, forsaken us for all time?" But the differences between the two bear scrutiny. The verse from Lamentations addresses God in the second person, following Zion's example in chapters 1 and 2 as she tried to get a response from God. In the context of the poem, the question has in fact been put into the mouth of the Zion figure, but it has been changed to the third person, addressing the reader (or hearer, given its liturgical setting) rather than God. Given the woman's description of her husband as having cast her off, turned away from her, and forgotten her, the lack of direct address to God (the "husband") is entirely appropriate; the mother of children is content only to describe her pain and abandonment to the reader.[12]

The most significant difference between Lamentations 5:20 and its citation in "The Mother of Children," however, is what comes after it: in Lamentations there is the continuing silence of God, but in Kallir's kinah there is a decisive and consoling response. "I have already answered your prayer of complaint," replies God, "as when I

dwelt crowned in your midst." There is in what follows this initial
line—as in Isaiah 49—a certain rhetorical overkill in God's response,
which utilizes the language of love and marriage from the biblical
book Song of Songs: first, in stanza 5, with regard to God's defeat of
Zion's enemies, and second, in stanza 6, with regard to God's promise never to reject Zion. While the language is taken from the Song
of Songs, as in Kallir's poem "Bound in Joy" (בשמחה אגודים),[13] it is
possible that the author has lifted the marriage theme from the book
of Isaiah. In Isaiah 54 Zion is told that "the one who created you will
espouse you," and that "the LORD has called you back as a wife forsaken (כאשה עזובה) and destitute." God's speech in the kinah ends
with the citation of Lamentations 5:20—albeit transformed in exactly the way that the rhetoric of Lamentations demanded: "I will not
abandon you, I will not forget you" (לא אעזבך ולא אשכחך).

God assures the Zion figure that her complaints have come to an
end and been swept away. But is that the case? While the poem certainly devotes great energy to providing God's response, it does little
to address the central complaint of Zion in the book of Lamentations: the fate of her children. This incongruence is only made more
acute by the opening phrase of the poem, where the Zion figure of
the kinah is called the "mother of children." In my judgment, this ep-
ithet modifies the complaints of Zion that follow it. Thus, Zion's accusation that God has abandoned her is less intended to restore a broken romantic relationship than to assure that her children have the
means to survive. God's reply seems to ignore this aspect of Zion's
speech, leading one to wonder whether her complaints really have
come to an end.

"Can It Be True?"

The next poem by Kallir to be considered in this chapter was also
intended for use in the Tisha b'Av liturgy. I will refer to it also by
its opening phrase, "Can It Be True?" The poem sustains for twenty-
two lines a tone of shock and disbelief, each line opening with
the conditional particle אם (pronounced 'im and usually translated
elsewhere as "if"). It is difficult to know how to render this particle,
but I think that Rosenfeld's choice in his translation of the first
line, "When (I think how) women could devour their own offspring . . . ," falls short of communicating the sheer horror and the

resulting sense that what is being described is very nearly unthinkable. My rendering as a dazed question attempts to preserve this sense.[14]

I noted in my treatment of "The Mother of Children" above that it is crucial to identify the exegetical context of the kinah. This poem is no different—in fact it mobilizes a verse from Lamentations in much the same structurally important way. But while "The Mother of Children" cited Lamentations 5:20, "Can It Be True?" cites Lamentations 2:20. And just as the previous poem overlapped significantly with its exegetical cousin in Isaiah 49, so does this poem overlap with the targum's treatment of Lamentations 2:20. While there are numerous biblical allusions in this poem, both from Lamentations and elsewhere, it is Lamentations 2:20 that inspires the poet's interpretive imagination. The verse is cited both in the poem's opening line and in its closing line. The first line of the poem reads, "Can it be true that women devour their offspring, the children they have cared for?" (אם תאכלנה נשים פרים). The line is an exact quote of the second clause of Lamentations 2:20, which was an important text for my reading of Lamentations in chapter two. In the biblical book this line constitutes Zion's response to the poet's urging for her to make one last attempt—"for the life of your infants" (על נפש עולליך; 2:19)—to get a response from God. The targum, of course, chose just this verse in which to supply the answer from God demanded by the rhetoric of Lamentations. As I noted, the answer it supplied—placed in the mouth of the Attribute of Justice—completely ignored both Zion's and the poet's concern for the survival of the children. Instead, one of Zion's lines (the third clause in the verse) is co-opted by the Attribute of Justice and pressed into service as a statement of Israel's guilt for the murder of Zechariah son of Iddo. Kallir's poem seems bent on making sure that this most central theme is not overlooked again, for what follows the initial citation of Lamentations 2:20 are nine lines devoted exclusively (and excruciatingly) to the suffering and cannibalization of children.

The descriptions that follow are quite graphic, drawing on, expanding, and adding to images from biblical Lamentations. But while the opening line from Lamentations 2:20 speaks of women devouring their own children, the rest of the kinah takes great care to mitigate their guilt. I pointed out in chapter five that in the targum's

treatment of this verse, the phrase "from starvation" was added to alleviate at least somewhat the negative image of these women.[15] It
may in fact be that Kallir had in mind this targumic expansion, for
the theme of starvation becomes the leitmotif of the nine lines that
follow. It is important to note that after line 1, there is no further
mention of the women themselves devouring their children, only
that they prepared them to be eaten. On the surface this does not offer much consolation, but it is likely that Kallir is making reference
to the midrashic tradition that the children were only prepared for
consumption *after* they had already died and even then only in order
to feed other children who still had a chance for survival. This reading is supported by the fact that the women are described as compassionate, and the children are described as "loved ones who were
carefully nurtured" (המדודים טפחים טפחים). Such a description
mobilizes more fully the reader's sympathy for the mothers, having
to make such a terrible choice. That they are forced to do so by
God—a theme of biblical Lamentations (see the discussion of 2:20
in chapter two)—is indicated in line 10, the end of the description
of the cannibalism.

> How could a woman be given a miscarrying womb
>   and dried-up breasts,
>   and a mother given children who sink toward death?

Here the poet makes allusion to the curse in Hosea of miscarrying
wombs[16] and dried-up breasts that is leveled against Israel. Hosea
9:14 reads:

> Give them—What will you give them YHWH?—
> Give them a miscarrying womb and dried-up breasts.[17]

The prophet Hosea then portrays God, in rage, as promising that,
"even if they do give birth, I will kill their precious offspring"
(9:16). It is clear that this belated poet has followed the lead of the
earlier poet of Lamentations in siding with the mothers and against
God.

After a digression in the central section of the poem (lines
11–17), which much like Lamentations 2:5–10 surveys the destruction wrought on the population as a whole, the poem returns
to the more specific theme of the horrible fate of the children. While

there is no mention of cannibalism in lines 18–22, the graphic nature of the children's death is if anything more gruesomely presented. Here one reads of "nine kabs" of children's brains being piled on rocks and of three hundred sucklings being impaled on one branch. The rhetoric is blatantly excessive in its portrayal of violent death; but it is so in order to counteract any theodic settlement whereby Israel's sufferings are somehow justified.

In light of the extended description of the ghastly fate of the children, the ultimate prose ending of the poem comes as a surprising anticlimax. Here one finds the second citation of Lamentations 2:20. The "holy spirit" (רוח הקדש) thunders: "'Can it be true that women devour their offspring?' (Lam. 2:20b), is proclaimed by Israel; but they refuse to proclaim 'Can it be that priest and prophet are slain in the temple?'" (Lam. 2:20c). Once again mirroring the targumic expansion, the biblical verse is here co-opted by the divine in order to counter the accusations by alluding to the murder of Zechariah. The answer is blatantly petty and certainly goes against the rhetorical intent of the poem as a whole. It is quite likely—given the fact that it is prose and that it occurs after the acrostic form has been completed—that it is an editorial addition meant to tone down the imprecatory nature of the *kinah*. But it is also possible that Kallir is using a play on words to veil some of the more heretical-sounding sentiments. The prose section begins with the holy spirit "confronting" (למולם) the מרעים (*mar'im*). But the word *mar'im* hosts no little ambiguity in its present context. It may well mean "wicked ones or evildoers" (from the Hebrew מרע). But it may also mean "those close to death" (from the Aramaic מרע).[18] Both potential meanings in fact fit quite well in the poem. The first would encourage an unproblematized reading of the divine response as a condemnation of the wicked behavior that has led to the present circumstances. The second would encourage a more subversive reading of the divine response as a further affliction of those described in such torturous detail by the poet. However one reads this particular word, the prose addition witnesses, like the targum, to the felt need for a response from God. Like the other texts I have considered in this study, these poems are not ideologically monolithic. They participate in orthodox theological presuppositions even when they venture to challenge such presuppositions. The dialogic nature of the poem,

whether the result of a reaction against the "heretical" poet or inscribed by the poet himself, produces a text in conflict with itself.

"Then in the Fullness of Her Grief"

The two kinot that I have considered thus far have, to varying de-
grees, mirrored the exegetical moves found in Second Isaiah and
Targum Lamentations, respectively. In the third poem by Kallir
to be treated—which I will call "Then in the Fullness of Her
Grief" (אז במלאת ספק)—there is a similar mirroring with regard to
Eikhah Rabbah. Here are assembled again the cast of characters from
petihta 24 (the opening homily that I considered at length in the previous chapter): the retreating Shekhinah, the angels, Jeremiah, the
patriarchs, and a mourning God. Missing only is Rachel, the import
of which I will explore below.[19]

The poem begins with "even the angels crying out in public"
(הן אראלם צעקו חוצה) on behalf of a woman who has "had her
full measure of grief." Jeremiah, coming away from the Temple
Mount (ארמון; cf. Lam. 2:5, 7), meets the once-beautiful woman,
now dressed in filthy clothes and with the appearance of a "demon"
(in Hebrew שד, šēd; likely a play on שד, šōd, meaning "ruined, devas-
tated"). The woman tells Jeremiah that she was once renowned for
her peace and repose, and that she was once the pride of Israel, from
Abraham to the seventy-one elders of the Sanhedrin. Jeremiah's advice to her is to repent, that she may no longer be called—quoting
from the biblical book that bears his name—"the faithless daughter"
(Jer. 31:22). To this point, we may note the similarities to a story in
the apocryphal book of 4 Ezra 9–10, where Ezra comes upon a
woman in a field whose clothes are rent and covered with ashes, as
she is mourning the loss of her son.[20] Ezra gives her advice similar to
Jeremiah's, to acknowledge the justice of God and to return to her
former station. In 4 Ezra the woman refuses to be consoled and is
suddenly transformed into the glorious city of Zion before Ezra's
eyes.[21]

The woman in Kallir's poem likewise refuses to be consoled for
the loss of her children: "How (איך) can I rejoice and sing aloud? My
infants (עוללי) are delivered into the hand of the enemy!" (see Lam.
1:7). She goes on to describe the destruction of the people as a
whole, culminating in the fleeing of her "beloved" (i.e., the Shekhi-

nah) from its dwelling place. It is the departure of the Shekhinah, we may recall, that precipitated God's own breakdown in the first of the stories from Eikhah Rabbah treated in chapter five. After this mention of the Shekhinah, the woman in the poem reveals herself clearly to the prophet as Zion, by a transposition of Lamentations 1:1: "She that was full of people—how lonely she sits." Combining this reference with imagery of sexual violation reminiscent of Lamentations 1:10, Kallir has the woman declare:

> My lovely tent has been ravaged
>   against my will.
> She that was full of people—
>   how lonely she sits.

In the final stanza of her speech she exhorts Jeremiah to pray to God on her behalf, that God might declare that "she has had enough." The imagined result of this, as Zion makes clear in her final line is that "he will deliver my children from the sword and from captivity" (ויציל בני מחרב ושביה). With this line there is another clear identification with Zion from Lamentations, for children given over to "captivity" and "the sword" is an explicit concern of Zion's. In Lamentations 1:5 the reader is told that "her infants" (עולליה) have gone into captivity (שבי), and in 1:18 Zion herself laments that boys and girls have gone into captivity (הלכו בשי). In 2:20–21 there is a conflation of these earlier verses, as Zion tells of her infants whom YHWH has afflicted (2:20) and of the girls and boys fallen "by the sword" (נפלו בחרב; 2:21).

As Zion is able to enlist the poet to intercede on her children's behalf in biblical Lamentations, so too Zion in the kinah is able to enlist Jeremiah (who in the eyes of Kallir is the poet of Lamentations) to intercede on behalf of her children. In stanza nine of the poem, Jeremiah thus entreats God: "You who are filled with compassion, show compassion as a father upon his son." Zion and the prophet succeed in getting a response from God, who cries out: "Woe to the father who has banished his son, and to the son who is not at his father's table!" With this exchange one is back squarely in the midst of petihta 24 of Eikhah Rabbah, where God compares God's self to "a man who had an only son, for whom he prepared a marriage canopy, but he died under it." And as God berates Jeremiah in the midrash for his lack of sympathy and sends him to summon "Abraham, Isaac, and Jacob, and Moses from their sepulchres, for they know how to weep," in the poem God admonishes Jeremiah likewise: "Arise Jeremiah! Why are you silent? Go summon the patriarchs and Aaron and Moses, let the shepherds come and raise a lament" (קינה). The poem ends with Jeremiah "roaring" outside the cave of Machpelah:

> Weep loudly, honored patriarchs!
> For your children are wandering, they are captives.

God's compassion has been aroused, as in the midrash, but the children remain in exile at the end of the poem.

The kinah, then, presents a "survival" of Lamentations that is in many ways similar to Eikhah Rabbah, but in the end is fundamentally transformed. The most striking difference, given her importance to the midrash, is the absence of Rachel. There, it was Rachel who finally succeeded in effecting God's promise to return her children. God's compassion is aroused in the kinah by the fate of the children, as it was in the first half of the petihta, but without Rachel "leaping into the fray," as she did at the end of the petihta, the children remain under threat. It may be that Kallir had in mind an earlier version of the midrashic story, which as we noted ended without the character of Rachel and without the restoration of the children. But there are clues I think that this was not the case. First, I would argue that Zion in effect stands in for the figure of Rachel in the midrash. Or perhaps it should be said that Zion "reemerges from" the figure of Rachel, since as I noted in chapter five Rachel is herself a cipher for Zion. On this reading, Kallir simply brings back the figure of Zion in a more explicit form. But like Rachel, Zion refuses to be comforted in Kallir's poem, even as she refused to be comforted in 4 Ezra. Second, if a trace of Rachel remains in the figure of Zion, a trace also remains in the figure of God. God's initial outburst of emotion, in which God compares the divine self to a father who has lost his son, preserves this trace. The final two lines of the stanza read:

> He cried out: Woe to the father who has banished his son,
> and woe to the son who is not at his father's table.

The choice of words (אינו, "he is not") to convey the absence of the son and the syntax of the final sentence, emphasizing that absence, cannot fail to bring to the reader's mind the similarly worded ending of Jeremiah 31:15:

> A cry is heard in Ramah,
>> lamentation and bitter weeping.
>
> Rachel weeping for her children.
>> She refuses to be comforted for her children;
>> for they are not.

It is just this verse, of course, that one finds at the end of *petihta* 24 in Eikhah Rabbah, followed, moreover, by a citation of Jeremiah 31:16, where the promise of the children's restoration is given. The poet thus preserves traces of the figure of Rachel as well as a trace of the promised return of the children. But he refrains from voicing such an explicit survival. Why? The answer may be that since he was writing for the liturgical context of Tisha b'Av, in which one deliberately refrained from hope, he felt the need to repress the ending of the *petihta*.[22] Having said this, we may note that all three of the *kinot* considered here are similar in that, while showing awareness of Zion's demand for the survival of her children, they are reticent to see it through.

The lack of a final and decisive survival in these poems points to a larger issue that has been in the background of this study from the beginning. That is, how the interpretive afterlife of Lamentations can valorize and attempt to meet the drive for survival therein without voicing a restoration that rings false to present circumstances of exile and diaspora, and without betraying Lamentations' witness to suffering by subsuming it in a happy ending. This is the paradox of the "poetics of survival." As I will show in the next chapter, it is just this question that has taken on tremendous import for contemporary readers of Lamentations.

The Liturgical Context of Kallir's Poetry

Before moving in the following chapter to the possibilities of survival for Lamentations in the contemporary era, I want to call attention to the turning point represented by the medieval *kinot* examined above. Earlier survivals of Lamentations—in Isaiah, the targum, and the midrash, as well as in 4 Ezra—were similar in imagining a final and decisive restoration of Zion's children. Each identified the need for a response to Zion's vehement accusations, and each provided that response in the form of an eschatological homecoming. With the poems of Kallir, however, one reaches another "stage of the afterlife"[23] of the book of Lamentations.

The new stage of survival for Lamentations is indicated both by the intentional absorption of previous survivals and by the refusal to ignore history in favor of eschatology. Earlier responses were presented as if nothing had come before and nothing would come after in the history of interpretation: this particular answer for this particular era and community is what mattered most. But the poems of Kallir evidence a self-conscious relationship with what has come before and an uncertainty about what will come after. With regard to what has come before, the kinot represent an end point, a symptom of the demise of the exegetical trajectory that I have followed in earlier chapters. By gathering together the fragments of these previous responses to the accusations of Zion and using them to construct new responses, Kallir calls attention to the fact that these erstwhile answers were finally inadequate. Although the drama of call and response is certainly "played out" (or reenacted) once more in the poetry of Kallir, just as certainly is the trajectory of survival "played out" (or expended) in these poems that can no longer imagine a triumphal celebration of reunion. But with regard to what follows, these poems open out toward an unknown future, one in which a felt absence is acknowledged but is nonetheless resisted. All this is to say that a "poetics of survival" has crystallized around these liturgical texts, a poetics that recognizes the need for a response to its precursive texts while also admitting that no response is ever final and comprehensive.

By reintroducing the qualifier "liturgical" to my description of these poems, I mean to call attention to the importance of Tisha b'Av as the context for this poetics of survival. Even as the kinot stand in the context of Tisha b'Av, so too does Tisha b'Av stand in the context of the Jewish liturgical calendar. By looking more closely at its place in the calendar, we may see how the poetics of survival have been absorbed into the cycle of the year. At the head of the year is Rosh Hashanah, the celebration of the New Year. The holiday is a time of new beginnings and is identified by tradition as the anniversary of the creation of the first human. So while the first month of the year according to the Bible is Nisan, the month of spring and Pesach, the cycle of festivals and fasts as lived by the liturgical community begins with the new creation on Rosh Hashanah.[24] But already in the first holiday of the year one finds the mixture of celebration and mourning, of praise and lament, that characterizes the year as a whole. For while Rosh Hashanah is a time of beginning and renewal, it is also a time of judgment and a call to repentance, leading after ten days to Yom Kippur, the day of atonement. The year progresses through various festivals and fasts: Sukkot, Hanukkah, the Fast of the Tenth of Tevet, Tu bi-Shvat, Purim, Pesach, Shavuot, and the Fast of the Seventeenth of Tammuz. At the end of the cycle comes Tisha b'Av, the Ninth of Av.

The fact that the liturgical year ends on Tisha b'Av both helps to explain the poetics of survival inscribed in the kinot of Kallir and itself reflects, I contend, the structural truncation of Lamentations that gave rise to the afterlife with which this study is concerned. As the medieval kinot tended to gather fragments of biblical and rabbinic texts and incorporate these fragments within themselves, so too did Tisha b'Av tend to gather fragments from destructions in the history of Judaism and absorb them into this single day of fasting and mourning. As tradition has it, Tisha b'Av was the day on which four momentous tragedies happened: the destruction of the first temple, the destruction of the second temple, the fall of Betar (the last stronghold of the Bar Kochba rebellion), and the plowing under of Jerusalem by the Romans. Added to these in later years was the expulsion of Jews from Spain in 1492. And as the medieval kinot represent an ending that also opens out toward the future, so too does Tisha b'Av not only stand at the end of the liturgical year but also opens out to something beyond that ending. Though the Fast of Tisha b'Av is the last event on the calendar, it does not actually mark the end of the year; for after the fasting is over and the laments have been voiced, there remains the rest of the month of Av and the entire month of Elul, which is filled with daily services of selichot (penitential prayers). The year lives on despite the deathly tenor of Tisha b'Av, though it refuses to move too quickly toward a happy ending or a festival of celebration. Instead what one encounters in the weeks following Tisha b'Av is a waiting—a waiting for the Messiah to come or, failing that, to begin the year all over again. Judaism did not end with the destruction of either the first or the second temple; there were those who survived and lived on in the periods of exile that followed. Neither does the cycle of festivals and fasts end with the destruction represented by Tisha b'Av; the year lives beyond it through its own period of exile.

What I find most striking about this truncated structure of the liturgical cycle is the way it reflects the similar structure of the book of Lamentations itself. On my reading of Lamentations, the book is primarily concerned to engender a response from God. In attempting to do so it employs many different rhetorical strategies and theological perspectives, though for the purposes of this study I have focused almost exclusively on the figure of Zion in chapters 1 and 2. But in the absence of any response, the book of Lamentations must finally end, leading not only to the historical exile suffered by Judah, but also to the exile of the word into the history of interpretation. So the biblical book and the liturgical fast each comes to the same inevitable nonending. Each demands and expects an answer, though neither will finally allow a provisional answer to stand. But as long as there remains someone to read the book and someone to do the fast, each will survive.

SEVEN

Survival under Threat: Contemporary Possibilities and Impossibilities

> But if the Jewish mind could be prepared for voluntary suffering, even the massacre I have imagined could be turned into a day of thanksgiving and joy that Jehovah had wrought deliverance of the race even at the hands of the tyrant. For the God-fearing, death has no terror.
>
> Mahatma Gandhi

> No survival in this death, but an implacable sur-death.
>
> Edmond Jabès

The above statement by Mahatma Gandhi, written in 1938 in response to what was then known of the Nazi persecution of European Jewry, is a statement about survival. Gandhi imagines a triumph of life beyond the borders of death, a transformation of massacre into thanksgiving and joy. The tone is unwavering in its confidence: "Death has no terror." Gandhi's vision of survival, in its refusal to admit the finality of death and in its resolute attempt to imagine deliverance by "Jehovah," fits well with the rhetoric of consolation and restoration that I have identified in the exegetical afterlife of Zion and her children. As we have seen, time and again in the history of the interpretation of the book of Lamentations the urge to supplement the biblical book is manifested by supplying the voice of God and thereby restoring the truncated dialogue between God and personified Zion. By providing the response that Zion demands, and by focusing that response on the unexpected and unexplainable survival of Zion's lost children, the texts that I have considered in the course of this book have also ensured the survival of Lamentations among later generations of readers. The book has remained a vital and generative piece of literature.

This survival of Lamentations—this piling on of texts that I have traced—has, however, come under threat in the modern period. The intense and imaginative exegetical impulse to supplement Lamentations 1 and 2 has all but died out; one looks in vain for recent poetic, literary, or theological works that attend to Zion's unanswered accusations to God. One is tempted to attribute this circumstance to the reduced presence of the biblical idiom in modern culture in general and modern Jewish culture in particular, a reduced presence that may be imagined either as a gradual fading away or, following David Roskies, a more intentional "antitraditionalist revolt."[1] No doubt this is partly responsible, yet it does not explain the numerous other biblical references in the works of modern writers such as Uri Zvi Greenberg, Amir Gilboa, Yehuda Amichai, Nelly Sachs, or Dan Pagis. To be sure, the Bible is often mobilized in ironic ways by these writers, but we know that this was the case in much "traditional" literature as well. No, there must be something more substantial to the absence of Lamentations in modern literary and theological discourse than just a reaction against the use of traditional sources. My own opinion is that this absence is attributable in large part to a fundamental misconstrual of the attitude toward suffering in Lamentations, and that this misconstrual is itself due to an unwarranted emphasis on the suffering man of chapter 3. Consider, for example, the following statement by Roskies about the need to fit suffering into an intelligible framework: "Hence, the pathetic attempts in Lamentations to awaken God's mercy, to insist that even suffering must be good (3:26–30), that both weal and woe proceed from the Word of God (3:38)."[2] Roskies appeals to chapter 3 to support this characterization of the tradition represented by Lamentations, but ignores the challenge that the figure of Zion poses to such a characterization. Likewise, the editors of a recent anthology of poems and stories on the Holocaust, entitled *Truth and Lamentation*, write: "If humility is the characteristic tone in traditional lamentation literature, a certain spiritual audacity characterizes the response of modern Jewish authors."[3] Again, the inadequacy of this statement to Zion's bold challenges to God is obvious. Yet the statement represents a ubiquitous but problematic assumption in much recent scholarship: namely, that so-called tradition is always and everywhere characterized by humility and a submissive attitude toward God, while audacity and challenges to God can be found only in modern, antitraditionalist writings. It is not surprising then that recent writers have steered clear of Lamentations, given this pervasive understanding of its theological potential. That this understanding presupposes a far too limited view of tradition should, in light of the texts examined in the chapters above, be clear.

And yet, as my study draws to a close and I ponder the possibilities for the survival of Lamentations in and beyond the twentieth century I find myself admitting that the project of restoration and consolation represented by Second Isaiah, Targum Lamentations, Eikhah Rabbah, and the kinot of Kallir, while vastly more complex and potentially subversive than one might expect, is no longer adequate. Edmond Jabès, in the second epigraph above, calls just this sort of project into question, substituting for the rhetoric of consolation a rhetoric of melancholia, of perpetual loss. The quote from Jabès— written at least partially in response to the Holocaust, as all of his work is[4]—offers a sobering alternative to the statement by Gandhi. For Jabès, death retains its terror and infiltrates the triumph represented by survival, leading not to an excess of life but an excess of death, a "sur-death." While Gandhi's statement may cohere with the history of interpretation of Lamentations, Jabès evokes the destitution and the default of God preserved in the book of Lamentations itself. Thus, by citing Jabès as an epigraph to my final chapter there is a sense in which I bring my study full-circle. We are back to the biblical book, with its unrelenting depiction of death, and we are back to the words of personified Zion in her final speech: "none survived and none escaped" (Lam. 2:22).

Alan Mintz has written that the function of Second Isaiah's prophecy is "to reconstruct the faculty of hearing, to recreate the conditions under which the reality of divine speech regains plausibility."[5] The characterization holds true for the other survivals of Lamentations considered up to this point as well, and it points to the crux of my uncertainty about the present possibilities for the survival of Lamentations: Is it possible to imagine recreating such conditions in the present context, particularly after the silence of God during the Holocaust? Can the representation of divine speech ever regain plausibility? Is it possible to imagine the triumphant return of Zion's children without betraying the memory of the one million children who did not return from Nazi death camps? Acknowledging these problems does not, however, lessen the urgency of Zion's demands that remain in Lamentations. Thus one faces more squarely the paradox only hinted at in Kallir's poetry: how to meet the drive for survival in Lamentations—to fill the unbearable whiteness of its nonending—in a way that does not ring false to the present historical situation.

One example how this might be done is found in Cynthia Ozick's short story "The Shawl."[6] This is the final "survival" of Lamentations that I will consider in this study, but unlike the previous examples, "The Shawl" is not explicitly presented as an interpretation of Lamentations. While Ozick has stated in a recent interview that she reads the Bible in Hebrew quite often, I am not entirely convinced that she consciously had Lamentations in mind as a subtext for the story.[7] Be that as it may, the echoes of Mother Zion and her threatened children are very much present, albeit transformed to an extent not yet encountered in this study. If the poetry of Kallir portended a certain dying out of the exegetical trajectory that I have identified, "The Shawl" counters this exhaustion with the possibility of a new instance of survival. Yet even as it allows for Lamentations to live beyond its borders, to live again in a new context, "The Shawl" nevertheless creates a narrative world in which the terms of survival set by its precursors become impossible to imagine. In my treatment of the literature of survival in chapter one I argued that a key element in such literature is the commingling of life and death. The texts I have considered to this point maintain this commingling, but work to emphasize the extravagance of life restored. "The Shawl" likewise maintains the intermixing of life and death, though finally conceding more to death than it does to life.

Possibilities for Survival in "The Shawl"

"The Shawl" opens with its three main characters—Rosa, Magda, and Stella—on a cold and barren march. The reader gradually learns that they are Jews on a march toward a Nazi concentration camp. Rosa is the mother of Magda, an infant as the story begins but a toddler by the end of it. Stella is Rosa's niece. Rosa has managed to keep Magda alive by hiding her in a shawl, nursing her until her milk runs dry, and then sharing her food when they are in a barracks. But Magda's survival is precarious.

> Rosa knew that Magda was going to die very soon; she should have been dead already, but she had been buried deep inside the magic shawl, mistaken there for the shivering mound of Rosa's breasts.[8]

Once in the camp, Rosa knows that it is only a matter of time until someone would inform on them, or someone "would steal Magda to eat her." In spite of these constant threats, Magda manages to survive, wrapped always in her shawl and sucking on it for the comfort no longer available from Rosa's breasts.

But one day, "Stella took the shawl away and made Magda die. Afterward Stella said: 'I was cold.'"[9] Magda wanders out of the barracks and into the open square, "with her little pencil legs scribbling this way and that, in search of the shawl." Rosa sees too late to stop Magda, who, silent until now, is howling in "the perilous sunlight of the arena."

> A tide of commands hammered in Rosa's nipples: Fetch, get, bring! But she did not know which to go after first, Magda or the shawl. If she jumped out into the arena to snatch Magda up, the howling would not stop, because Magda would still not have the shawl; but if she ran back into the barracks to find the shawl, and if she found it, and if she came after Magda holding it and shaking it, then she would get Magda back.[10]

Opting for the latter, Rosa enters the barracks, tears the shawl away from Stella, and runs into the arena, holding it aloft for Magda to see.

> Far off, very far, Magda leaned across her air-fed belly, reaching out with the rods of her arms. She was high up, elevated, riding someone's shoulder. But the shoulder that carried Magda was not coming toward Rosa and the shawl, it was drifting away, the speck of Magda moving more and more into the smoky distance.[11]

Magda has been discovered and is carried by a guard toward the electrified fence. The final paragraph of the story reads:

> All at once Magda was swimming through the air. The whole of Magda traveled through loftiness. She looked like a butterfly touching a silver

vine. And the moment Magda's feathered round head and her pencil legs
and balloonish belly and zigzag arms splashed against the fence, the steel
voices went mad in their growling, urging Rosa to run and run to the
spot where Magda had fallen from her flight against the electrified fence;
but of course Rosa did not obey them. She only stood, because if she ran
they would shoot, and if she tried to pick up the sticks of Magda's body
they would shoot, and if she let the wolf's screech ascending now
through the ladder of her skeleton break out, they would shoot; so she
took Magda's shawl and filled her own mouth with it, stuffed it in and
stuffed it in, until she was swallowing up the wolf's screech and tasting
the cinnamon and almond depth of Magda's saliva; and Rosa drank
Magda's shawl until it dried.[12]

So the story ends, with a bereaved mother squelching the cry of grief
and shock at witnessing the murder of her child.

What then are the connections between this story and Lamentations? At the thematic level, with its emphasis on the mother-child
relationship, the threat of an enemy, and the hints of cannibalism,
"The Shawl" bears a marked resemblance to the book of Lamentations. But is there more than a general correspondence of themes
that would justify my claiming it as a post-Holocaust instance of the
"survival" of the biblical book? Attention to the details of the story
suggests that there is a more direct intertextual relationship to be
teased out.

There are, for example, two *Leitworten* in the story, key words repeated for emphasis, that point the reader to Lamentations. The first
of these to be encountered is "pity." The absence of pity is repeated
three times in the description of the characters' situation: "They
were in a place without pity, all pity was annihilated in Rosa, she
looked at Stella's bones without pity."[13] The English word "pity" has
a semantic field in biblical Hebrew that includes the roots חמל
(ḥāmal), נחם (niḥam), and רחם (riḥam). Just as "pity" is a *Leitwort* in "The
Shawl," two of these three words for pity are *Leitworten* in Lamentations 1 and 2. The notion of the absence of pity in the face of desperate suffering most immediately recalls the repeated refrain in
chapter 1 that Zion has no one to "comfort/pity" (niḥam) her. In
chapter 2 the poet employs ḥāmal to express the lack of pity from the
LORD: the reader is told in 2:17 that the LORD "has destroyed with-

out pity," and in 2:21 that the LORD has slaughtered boys and girls "without pity." Thus the opening chapters of Lamentations and "The Shawl" are both concerned with constructing in the mind of the reader a world in which all hope of pity and comfort are extinguished.

The second common *Leitwort* is the "arena" or "the square," encountered in the Ozick story when Magda stumbles out of the barracks in search of her shawl.[14] By the time Rosa sees her, "already Magda was in the square outside." Ozick deftly contrasts the peril of the arena outside with the safety of the shawl inside the barracks:

> It was the roll-call arena. Every morning Rosa had to conceal Magda under the shawl against a wall of the barracks and go out and stand in the arena with Stella and hundreds of others, sometimes for hours, and Magda, deserted, was quiet under the shawl, sucking on her corner.[15]

It is into the arena that Magda stumbles out, "swaying on her pencil legs," and it is in the arena that she dies. The semantic range in biblical Hebrew of "arena" or "square" is primarily constituted by the two words רחוב (r^eḥob) and חוץ (ḥûṣ), both of which occur in Lamentations 2, both of which are explicitly named as the place where Zion's children are dying. The first, r^eḥob, is repeated twice in 2:11–12, where the poet breaks down in verse 11 over the "babes and sucklings [who] falter in the squares of the city" (2:11). Verse 12 reads:

> They falter like the wounded,
>   in the squares of the town,
> as their life runs out
>   in the bosom of their mother.

The citation of this verse demonstrates the subtle complexity with which "The Shawl" echoes the biblical book. It does so not only in the choice of the square as the place of the children's death, but also in the description of how the children make their way through the square. In "The Shawl," Magda sways on perilously thin legs: she "flopped onward with her little pencil legs scribbling this way and that," and she "falters" in the sunlight of the arena. The imperiled children are presented in this same way in Lamentations, where the verb עטף (ʿāṭap), repeated twice and usually translated as "languished," can mean "to be faint" or "to falter." The image of Magda stumbling to her death in the square recalls the stumbling of Zion's children to their death in the rᵉḥob.

The web of correlation extends even further in this verse. In a key paragraph of "The Shawl" (partially quoted above), Ozick sets up a structural opposition between the safety of the shawl and the threat of the open square. The shawl itself stands in for the bosom of Rosa: it is a surrogate source of nourishment and safety when Rosa's breasts have given all they can or when Rosa is unable to carry Magda with her, e.g., into the roll-call arena. Thus when Rosa enters the square, she has to "conceal Magda under the shawl." And the reader is told twice that "since the drying up of Rosa's nipples," only the shawl could keep Magda quiet and therefore safe. Earlier in the story, the identification of shawl with bosom is made even more explicit when it is said that Magda would have died had she not been "buried away deep inside the magic shawl, mistaken there for the shivering mound of Rosa's breasts."[16] I explore this at length because of the fact that just at the key point of Lamentations 2:12, with which "The Shawl" has already displayed a strong correspondence, one reads that the children's lives are running out "in the bosom (חיק, ḥêq) of their mother." What is astonishing, in light of the connotations of the bosom/shawl in Ozick's story, is that in the Bible ḥêq quite often indicates a "fold of garment at the breast," or in other words, a shawl (Ex. 4:6–7; Prov. 6:27; 16:33). Furthermore, it serves as a place of concealment, as in Proverbs 21:14 and Job 23:12. Thus the shawl as a surrogate bosom and place of concealment may also be seen as an echo of Lamentations.

Beyond these detailed correspondences between the biblical book and Ozick's short story, there are larger thematic similarities, such as the threat of cannibalism, occurring in Lamentations 2:20 and 2:22, and later in 4:10 as well. In "The Shawl" it is no less present. Rosa is primarily concerned with Stella's designs on Magda:

> Rosa thought how Stella gazed at Magda like a young cannibal. And the time that Stella said "Aryan," it sounded to Rosa as if Stella had really said "Let us devour her."[17]

But she is also afraid that "one day someone, not even Stella, would steal Magda to eat her." Of course the largest theme of all, in both Lamentations 1 and 2 and in "The Shawl," is the frustrated attempt of a mother to keep her children alive in the face of a violent and powerful enemy.

Melancholia and the Impossibility of Mourning

If it is true that "The Shawl" takes up the concerns of Zion for the survival of her children and makes those concerns its own, it is no less true that the survival represented by "The Shawl" has been radically transformed. Long gone are the buoyancy of Second Isaiah and the promises of the targum and the midrash. Missing too is the advocacy of Jeremiah, roaring on behalf of the children as we saw in the kinah "In the Fullness of Her Grief." And, of course, most palpably absent is the voice of God. The only response to Magda's death in "The Shawl" is Rosa's "wolf's screech," a screech cut short by filling her mouth with Magda's beloved shawl. So the nonending of the story is not unlike the nonending of the book of Lamentations: a mother fails in her attempts to keep her children alive, and the reader is left to fill the silence of nonresponse, the white space of the final page, as best as she or he can. In this way, "The Shawl" is more nearly akin to the biblical book than are those supplements explicitly concerned with its interpretation. The two works stand as melancholic bookends at either end of a long and desperate history of interpretation.

In characterizing Lamentations and "The Shawl" as melancholic, I refer back to a phrase from the opening of this chapter, where I described the epigraph by Edmond Jabès as representing a "rhetoric of melancholia." The phrase needs unpacking. In Freud's original treatment of melancholia in 1917, he attempted to distinguish between mourning and melancholia. Though he begins by admitting that "the correlation of melancholia and mourning seems justified by the general picture of the two conditions," and that they may well be the product of "the same influences," he contends that, unlike mourning, melancholia is to be considered "a pathological disposition."[18] Freud writes that although it is true that "mourning involves grave departures from the normal attitude to life," we may "rely on its being overcome after a certain lapse of time."[19] This overcoming, the work of mourning, proceeds by way of reality testing, which shows that the loved object no longer exists and that attachments to the object must be withdrawn. Resistance follows, but eventually "reality gains the day," and "when the work of mourning is completed the ego becomes free and uninhibited again" and thus able to attach itself to a new object.[20] Melancholia, on the other hand, is precisely the failure of the work of mourning; it is the inability of the ego to overcome the loss of the object, the inability to break off the tie, no matter how much reality is tested and found wanting.

Freud's structure of mourning—presence/loss of presence/restored presence—is in fact the converse of the history of interpretation of the book of Lamentations that I have traced in this study. Rather than absence surrounded by presence, one finds destitution and default at both ends of a long and desperate attempt to stave off the melancholia of sustained absence. Previous survivals of Lamentations have certainly honored the mourning of Mother Zion; indeed they have repeatedly taken it to be of such importance that it must not go unanswered. In their responses, these texts mirror the completion of mourning described by Freud. They imagine that Zion's mourning has been accomplished and that the new object, or the object restored, has replaced the original loss. To use Gandhi's words, the massacre, though taken to be real, has been transformed into thanksgiving and joy. Enclosing these survivals, however, is the "sur-death" represented by both Lamentations and "The Shawl," which proclaim, instead of the completion of mourning, the impossibility of mourning. By this I do not mean that mourning does not exist for these two texts; it manifestly does. Rather, I mean to suggest that mourning may prove *impossible to accomplish*, to be done with.

The impossibility of mourning in this case does not, contra Freud, imply a pathological state, nor even one of resignation, since the *force* of mourning derives precisely from its renunciation. In a recent article, Jacques Derrida writes that "the force of mourning develops its maximal intensity, so to speak, only at the mad moment of decision, at the point of its absolute interruption, there where *dynamis* remains virtuality."[21] Derrida argues that one thus works *at* mourning both as an object and as a resource, "working at mourning as one would speak of a painter working at a painting but also of a machine working at such and such an energy level."[22] Melancholia is this perpetual state of interruption, and as such it preserves mourning as force, as virtuality. Melancholia impugns both an optimism that imagines to have paid its debt to loss, as well as a nihilism that acknowledges no debt to begin with. So these two bookends of destitution trade in absence and abandonment, but an absence that is felt and an abandonment that is resisted.

If the voice of God is no longer plausible, as it clearly is not in "The Shawl," can the story be said to meet the criteria to which I have appealed throughout this study? That is, am I justified in considering this story to be a "survival" of Lamentations in the same way as the other texts treated above? The answer is yes, I think, so long as one recognizes in the story a more limited survival, a survival under threat. For as Elaine Kauvar has pointed out, while "the magic shawl" was unable to keep Magda alive indefinitely, it was able to save Rosa's life: "the shawl, which once nourished the infant, now stifles its mother's screams . . . that will bring instant death."[23] Like Mother Zion, Rosa survives to lament the children that did not. It is a survival, to be sure, but one that is random and infinitely precarious. It is also, perhaps, the only survival possible in our present interpretive horizon.

The Death of Lamentations

So the figure of Zion survives, as does the book of Lamentations. Text after text has answered Lamentations, but none have replaced it. Zion's most recent incarnation as Rosa witnesses to the unrelenting absence at its center that defines the book of Lamentations and continues to demand that the suffering of children be addressed, even as such absence stands as a critique of every attempt to do so. There is a final irony, appropriate for closing this study, in the fervent hope of traditional Jews that Lamentations will not survive after all. Naomi Seidman tells the following story:

> In a certain small town in Poland, right after they broke the fast, the Jews would light an enormous bonfire. They would throw the Tisha B'av liturgy with all its sad poems about the destruction of the Temple into the fire and dance and sing the midsummer night away.[24]

The ever-recurrent hope is that, before the next Tisha b'Av, the messiah will come and suffering will cease and there will be no longer any need for lamenting. Until that happens, the afterlife of Lamentations will undoubtedly continue.

APPENDIX

Three Kinot of Eleazar ben Kallir

1. The Mother of Children

The mother of children moan like a dove,	אם הבנים כיונה מנהמת
She mourns in her heart and complains out loud,	בלב מתאוננת ובפה מתרעמת
She cries bitterly, calls out desparately,	גועה בבכי ובמר נואמת
She sheds tears, is silent, is stunned.	דמעות מזלת ודוממת ונדהמת
"My husband has abandoned me, and turned away from me.	השליכני בעלי וסר מעלי
He has not remembered my love as a bride.	ולא זכר אהבת כלולי
He has scattered me and dispersed me away from my land.	זרני ופזרני מעל גבולי
He has allowed all my tormentors to rejoice over me.	חדה עלי כל תוללי
He has cast me off as one unclean, banishing me from his presence.	טרפני כנדה ומפניו הדיחני
He has harshly ensnared me, and given me no respite.	יקשני בכבד ולא הניחני
He has chastised me until my eyes are worn out.	כלו עיני בתוכחות וכחני
Why has he forsaken me forever, forgotten about me?"	למה לנצח עזבני שכחני

145

"Why do you cry out to me, my dove,   מה תתאונני עלי יונתי
Blossom of delight in my garden?   נטע חמד ערוגת גנתי
Already I have answered your prayer,   שיח פלוליך כבר עניתי
As when I dwelt crowned in your midst.   עטור בך כאז חיתי

I have turned to you in great   פניתי אליך ברחמי הרבים
    compassion.
I am marching through the gate of   צעוד בשער בת רבים
    Bath Rabbim.
Though your enemies were numerous,   קמיך אשר עליך מתרבים
I shook them until they disappeared   רעשתי היות כעשו כבים
    like smoke.

My dark one, I will never desert you.   שחורתי לעד לא אזנחך
I shall again reach out my hand   שנית אוסיף יד ואקחך
    to take you.
Your complaints have ended,   תמו וספו דברי וכוחך
    they are no more.
My perfect one, I will not forsake   תמתי לא אעזבך ולא אשכחך
    you and I will not forget you."

2. Can It Be True?

Can it be true that women   אם תאכלנה נשים פרים עללי טפחים
    devour their offspring, infants
    they have cared for?

Can it be true that compassionate   אם תבשלנה נשים רחמניות ילדיהן
    women boiled their children,   המדודים טפחים טפחים
    whom they have so carefully
    nurtured?

Can it be true that their locks were   אם תגזנה פאת ראשם ותקשרנה
    taken as trophies and tied to   לסוסים פורחים
    the horses of the enemy?

Can it be true that the tongue of   אם תדבק לשון יונק לחך
    the suckling cleaves to his   בצמאון צחיחים
    palate from deathly thirst?

How could one woman say to   אם תהמנה זו לעמת זו בואי ונבשל
    another, "Come, let us boil   את בנינו צורחים
    our shrieking children"?

How could one woman bargain with another, "Give me your son," and he was already cut up and hid away?

אם תועדנה זו לזו תני בנך והוא חבוי מנתח נתחים

Can it be that the flesh of the fathers is prepared for the children in ditches and caves?

אם תזמין בשר אבות לבנים במערות ושיחים

Were the swollen bodies of the daughters clasped to the breast of their mothers?

אם תחיבנה הבנות אל חיק אמתם נתפחים

Can it be that the spirits of the dead infants hover over their bodies in the squares of the city?

אם תטסנה רוחות עוללים ברחבות קריה תפוחים

How could a woman be given a miscarrying womb and dried-up breasts, and a mother given children who sink toward death?

אם תיקרנה בשכול רחם וצמוק שדים ואם על בנים שחים

Have eight hundred armor bearers fallen and decayed in the desert?

אם תכשלנה שמונה מאות מגנים בערב אלוחים

How their breathing became inflamed, and their stomachs distended.

אם תלחטנה רוחם במיני מלוחים ונודות נפוחים

How a thousand were reduced by exhaustion to a hundred, then to ten, and to one.

אם תמעטנה מאלף מאה וממאה עשרה עד אחד למפחים

How eighty thousand young priests fled to the temple for safety.

אם תנסנה למסך היכל שמונים אלף כהנים פרחים

Were they really all burnt, like the cuttings from a thorn bush?

אם תשרפנה שם כל-אותם הנפשות כקוצים כסוחים

Should the necks of eighty thousand priests be broken for the shedding of innocent blood?

אם תערפנה על דם נקי שמונים אלף כהנים משוחים

How the wounded were swollen by the smell of the produce of the grass.

אם תפחנה נפשות מדקרים מריח תנבות שיחים

Can it be true that nine kabs of
children's brains were piled on
one stone?

אם תצברנה על אבן אחת תשעה
קבין מוחי ילדים מנחים

Can it be true that three hundred
sucklings were impaled on a
single branch?

אם תקענה שלש מאות יונקים על
שוכה אחת מתוחים

Should tender and delicate women
be in fetters before the chief
executioner?

אם תראינה רכות וענוגות כבולות
על יד רב הטבחים

Should the daughters of kings lie
in the garbage heap?

אם תשכבנה בין שפתים בנות
מליכים משבחים

Should young men and young
women die from a parching
thirst?

אם תתעלפנה הבתולות והבחורים
בצמאון צחיחים

ורוח הקדש למולם מרעים הוי על כל שכני הרעים
מה שהקראם מודיעים ואת אשר עשו לא מודעים
אם תאכלנה נשים פרים משמיעים אם יהרג
במקדש אדני כהן לא משמיעים

The Holy Spirit confronts the wicked ones: "Woe to all my evil
neighbors! They proclaim the fate they brought, but do not announce
what they themselves have done. They proclaim: 'Can it be true that
women devour their offspring?'; but they refuse to proclaim: 'Can it be
that priest and prophet are slain in the temple of the Lord?'"

3. Then in the Fullness of Her Grief

Then in the fullness of her grief—
  the one beautiful as Tirzah—

אז במלאת ספק יפה כתרצה

The attending angels cried aloud.

הן אראלם צעקו חוצה

The son of Hilkiah came from the
Temple Mount,

בן חלקיהו מארמון כיצא

And he found the beautiful woman
in filthy clothes.

אשה יפת תאר מנולת מצא

"I charge you—in the name of
God and humanity,

גוזרני עליך בשם אלהים ואדם

Are you a demon among demons
or a human being?

אם שד לשדים את או לבני אדם

Your beautiful form is like flesh
and blood,

דמות יפיך כבשר ודם

But the dread and fear of you can
only be that of angels!"

פחדך ויראתך כמלאכים לבדם

"I am neither a demon nor a
monster,

הן לא שד אני ולא גלם פחת

I was known for my elegance
and repose,

ידועה הייתי בשובה ונחת

I belonged to the three and to the
seventy-one

והן לשלוש אני ולשבעים ואחד

To twelve, to sixty, and to one.

לשנים עשר וששים ואחד

The one was Abraham,

זה האחד אברהם היה

And three were the patriarchs.

ובן השלושה אבות שלישיה

The twelve were the tribes of the
LORD,

חק שנים עשר הן הן שבטי יה

And the sixty the myriads, and the
seventy-one were the elders of
the LORD."

וששים רבוא ושבעים ואחד
סנהדרי יה

"Heed my advice and repent.

סעמי הקשיבי ועשי תשובה

Since you were once so esteemed,

יען היותך כל כך חשובה

It is right for you to exult and
rejoice in goodness,

יפה ליך בעלץ ולשמח בטובה

And you will no longer be called
the faithless daughter."

ולא תקרא עוד בת השובבה

"How can I rejoice, how can I sing
out loud?

כי איך אשמח וקולי מה אריম

My infants have been given into
the hands of the enemy,

הן עוללי נתנו ביד צרים

My prophets are beaten and
dragged away,

לקו נביאי והנם מגרים

My kings and princes are in exile,
and my priests in chains.

גלו מלכי ושרי וכהני בקולרים

Because of my sins, my holy place
is desolate.

מלון מקדשי בעווני נבדד

My beloved was driven from it
and fled.

דודי מאז רח וידד

My lovely tent is ravaged.

נעם אהלי בעל־כרחי שדד

She that was full of people, how
she sits alone.

רבתי עם איכה ישבה בדד

Pray to your god, prophet Jeremiah,
On behalf of the one who is storm-
    tossed, flogged, and afflicted.
Until God notices and says, 'Enough!'
And he will save my children from
    captivity and the sword."

סיח לאלהיך נביא ירמיה
בעד סערה מכה עניה

עד יענה אל ויאמר דיה
ויציל בני מחרב ושביה

He interceded before his creator:
"You who are full of pity, have pity
    as a father upon his son."
And God cried out: "Woe to the
    father who has banished his son,
And to the son who is not at his
    father's table.

פלל תחנה לפני קונו
מלא רחמים רחם כאב על בנו

צעק אוי לאב שהגלה נינו

וגם אוי לבן שבשלחן אב אינו

Arise Jeremiah, why are you silent
Go and call for the patriarchs, and
    for Aaron and Moses.
Let the shepherds come and raise
    a lament,
For desert wolves have devoured
    the lamb."

קום לך ירמיה למה תחשה
לך קרא לאבות ואהרן ומשה

רועים יבואו קינה להנשא

כי זאבי ערב טרפו את השה

Then the prophet Jeremiah roared
Outside Machpelah like a lion:
"Wail loudly, honored patriarchs;
For your children are wandering,
    they are captives."

שואג היה ירמיה הנביא
על מכפלה נוהם כלביא
תנו קול בבכי אבות הצבי
תעו בניכם הרי הן בשבי

Notes

Introduction

1. Unless otherwise indicated, all translations from the Hebrew of the biblical text are my own.

2. Delbert Hillers, *The Anchor Bible Commentary on Lamentations*, 2d ed. (Garden City, N.Y.: Doubleday, 1992), 122.

3. Jeffrey Tigay, "Lamentations," in *The Encyclopaedia Judaica* (Jerusalem: Keter Publishing Co., 1972), 1375.

4. Especially representative of the focus on chapter 3 are the following oft-cited works: Max Haller, *Die fünf Megilloth* (Tübingen: J. C. B. Mohr, 1940); Artur Weiser, *Klagelieder* (Göttingen: Vandenhoeck & Ruprecht, 1958); Hans-Joachim Kraus, *Klagelieder (Threni)*, 2d ed. (Neukirchen: Neukirchen Verlag, 1962); Brevard Childs, *Introduction to the Old Testament as Scripture* (Philadelphia: Fortress Press, 1979); Renate Brandscheidt, *Gotteszorn und Menschenleid: Die Gerichtsklage des leidenden Gerechten in Klgl 3* (Trier: Paulinus-Verlag, 1983); and Hillers, *Lamentations*. For the argument that the suffering man of chapter 3 is not nearly so submissive as interpreters have portrayed him, see the important new commentary by Kathleen M. O'Connor in *The New Interpreter's Bible* (Nashville: Abingdon Press, 1999).

5. A notable exception is Hedwig Jahnow's monograph *Das hebräische Leichenlied im Rahmen der Völkerdichtung* (Giessen: Verlag von Alfred Töpelmann, 1923), which because of its forceful argument for the connection between the book of Lamentations and the *Gattung* of the funeral dirge is ubiquitous in the literature.

6. Hillers, *Lamentations*, 6.

7. Alan Mintz, *Hurban: Responses to Catastrophe in Hebrew Literature* (New York: Columbia University Press, 1984), 3.

8. Ibid., 32.

9. Ibid., 33.

10. Ibid., 38–39.

11. Justin then takes this reference to breath to refer to the human nostrils, which take the shape of a cross when one looks to the sky. My thanks to Tim S. F. Horner for the Justin comment.

12. Walter F. Adenay, *The Lamentations of Jeremiah* (London: Hodder and Stoughton, 1895),182.

13. W. P. Merrill, "Lamentations," in *The Interpreter's Bible*, vol. 6, ed. G. A. Buttrick et al. (Nashville: Abingdon Press, 1956), 7.

14. Ibid., 23.

15. S. Paul Re'emi, *The Theology of Hope: A Commentary on the Book of Lamentations* (Grand Rapids: Eerdman's Press, 1984), 99.

16. Commenting on 3:39, Kraus writes: "Er weist ihr Murren (wortlich: sich in Klage ergehen) ab."

17. Robert Gordis, *The Song of Songs and Lamentations: A Study, Modern Translation, and Commentary* (New York: Ktav, 1974), 126.

18. Brandscheidt, *Gotteszorn und Menschenleid*, 212.

19. Paul Wayne Ferris Jr., *The Genre of Communal Lament in the Bible and the Ancient Near East* (Atlanta: Scholars Press, 1992), 146.

20. Brandscheidt, *Gotteszorn und Menschenleid*, 231.

21. Ferris, *Genre of Communal Lament*, 145–46.

22. Norman K. Gottwald, *Studies in the Book of Lamentations* (London: SCM Press, 1954), 62.

23. Otto Plöger, *Die fünf Megilloth* (J. C. B. Mohr, 1969), 161: "In einem Klagelied hat die Klage selbst, mag sie noch so ausführlich sein, keine selbständige Bedeutung."

24. Re'emi, *Theology of Hope*, 101.

25. Ibid., 106.

26. Mintz, *Hurban*, 36.

27. Hillers, *Lamentations*, 122.

28. Brandscheidt, *Gotteszorn und Menschenleid*, 36.

29. Cited in Hillers, *Lamentations*, 123.

30. Gottwald, *Studies*, 104–5.

31. Ibid., 107.

32. Claus Westermann, *Lamentations: Issues and Interpretation* (Minneapolis: Augsburg Fortress, 1994), 81.

33. Ibid., 78.

34. Ibid., 81.

35. Ibid., 92–93.

36. Ibid., 89–93.

37. Ibid., 116.

38. Ibid., 121.

39. Ibid., 132–34.

40. Ibid., 117.

41. Ibid., 154.

42. Ibid., 155.

43. Ibid., 127–28.

44. Ibid., 127.

45. Ibid., 157.

46. Iain Provan, Lamentations, New Century Bible Commentary (Grand Rapids: Eerdman's Press, 1991), 22–23.

47. Ibid., 84.

48. Ibid., 23.

49. F. W. Dobbs-Allsopp, Weep, O Daughter of Zion: A Study of the City-Lament Genre in the Hebrew Bible (Rome: Editrice Pontificio Instituto Biblico), 28.

50. I discuss the issue of genre in Lamentations more fully in chapter two.

51. Dobbs-Allsopp, Weep, O Daughter of Zion, 85.

52. Ibid., 54.

53. In a more recent article, "Tragedy, Tradition, and Theology in the Book of Lamentations," Journal for the Study of the Old Testament 74 (1997): 29–60, Dobbs-Allsopp moves from a comparative perspective to a literary-theological analysis of Lamentations as tragedy. The publication of his commentary on Lamentations in the Interpretation series, currently in progress, will undoubtedly extend these insights further.

54. Westermann, Lamentations, 81.

Chapter One

1. Anne Frank, Diary of a Young Girl, trans. B. M. Mooyaart-Doubleday (New York: Random House, 1952), 211.

2. Jacques Derrida, "Living On: Borderlines," in Deconstruction and Criticism, Harold Bloom et al. (New York: Seabury Press, 1979), 103.

3. Jean-François Lyotard, "The Survivor," in Toward the Postmodern (Atlantic Highlands, N.J.: Humanities Press, 1993), 144.

4. Primo Levi, Survival in Auschwitz, trans. S. Woolf (New York: Collier, 1961), 4.

5. Jean Améry, At the Mind's Limit: Contemplations by a Survivor on Auschwitz and Its Realities, trans. S. Rosenfeld and S. P. Rosenfeld (New York: Schocken Press, 1986), xiv.

6. Terrence Des Pres, The Survivor: An Anatomy of Life in the Death Camps (Oxford: Oxford University Press, 1976), 49.

7. The phrase "versions of survival" comes from the title of Langer's book Versions of Survival: The Holocaust and the Human Spirit (Albany: State University of New York Press, 1982).

8. Des Pres, The Survivor, v.

9. Ibid., 191.

10. Robert J. Lifton, Death in Life: Survivors of Hiroshima (New York: Simon and Schuster, 1967), 6–7.

11. Langer, Versions of Survival, 12.

12. For the purposes of this study I define the Holocaust as the attempted extermination of European Jewry by Nazi Germany. I am not unaware of the problems raised by such a definition, especially in its exclusion of non-Jews who also died at the hands of the Nazis, often side by side with Jews in concentration camps. It does seem, however, that Jews occupied a unique position in Nazi racial ideology and that therefore the planned extermination of Jews may be

treated as a phenomenon that is qualitatively different from the murder of other groups for political, economic, or other reasons. The one exception to this may well be the Nazi attitude toward and treatment of Gypsies. On the debate over these issues, see esp. Steven Katz, "The 'Unique' Intentionality of the Holocaust," in *Post-Holocaust Dialogues: Critical Studies in Modern Jewish Thought* (New York: New York University Press, 1983), 287—317; and Yehudah Bauer, "The Place of the Holocaust in Contemporary History," in *Holocaust: Religious and Philosophical Implications*, ed. J. Roth and M. Berenbaum (New York: Paragon Press, 1984), 16—42.

13. Victor Frankl, *Man's Search for Meaning: An Introduction to Logotherapy*, trans. I. Lasch (New York: Washington Square Press, 1963), 114.

14. Ibid., 179.

15. Bruno Bettelheim, *The Informed Heart: Autonomy in a Mass Age* (New York: Avon, 1960), 34.

16. Robert J. Lifton and Eric Olson, *Living and Dying* (New York: Bantam Books, 1975), 121.

17. Améry, *At the Mind's Limit*, 16.

18. Des Pres, *The Survivor*, 55.

19. Langer, *Versions of Survival*, 8.

20. Ibid., 65. See also Langer's more recent books, *Admitting the Holocaust* (Oxford: Oxford University Press, 1995); and *Preempting the Holocaust* (New Haven: Yale University Press, 1998).

21. Walter Benjamin, "Die Aufgabe des Übersetzers," in *Gesammelte Schriften* (Frankfurt am Main: Suhrkamp Verlag, 1972), 4:1.

22. Susan Handelman, *Fragments of Redemption: Jewish Thought and Literary Theory in Benjamin, Scholem, and Levinas* (Bloomington: Indiana University Press, 1991), 29.

23. Paul de Man, *The Resistance to Theory* (Minneapolis: University of Minnesota Press, 1986), 103.

24. Unless otherwise noted, I will refer to the English translation of Benjamin's essay found in Walter Benjamin, *Illuminations*, trans. H. Zohn (New York: Schocken Press, 1968), 70—82.

25. Ibid., 70.

26. Ibid.

27. Walter Benjamin, "Goethe's Elective Affinities," in *Selected Writings*, vol. 1, 1913—1926, ed. M. Bullock and M. Jennings (Cambridge: Harvard University Press, Belknap Press, 1996), 298.

28. Ibid., 299.

29. Benjamin, "Task of the Translator," 72.

30. Ibid., 71.

31. Benjamin, "Die Aufgabe des Übersetzers," 10—11.

32. Benjamin, "Task of the Translator," 79.

33. Ibid., 74.

34. Ibid., 80.

35. Ibid., 79.

36. See Gershom Scholem, *Major Trends in Jewish Mysticism* (New York: Schocken Books, 1941), 265–68, on the kabbalistic doctrine of *shevirat ha-kelim*, especially as worked out in the thought of the sixteenth-century mystic Isaac Luria. While scholars have tended to assume that Benjamin was influenced by Scholem's work in kabbalah, there is also the distinct possibility that Scholem's explication of kabbalistic thought was influenced by his conversations with Benjamin (see Handelman, *Fragments of Redemption*, 25–29). On the relationship between the two men, see Scholem's own account in *Walter Benjamin: The Story of a Friendship* (New York: Schocken Press, 1981), and Handelman's account in part 1 of *Fragments of Redemption*.

37. John Lechte, "Walter Benjamin," in *Fifty Key Contemporary Thinkers: From Structuralism to Postmodernity* (London: Routledge Press, 1994), 205.

38. Peggy Kamuf, introductory comments to an excerpt from "Living On: Borderlines," in *A Derrida Reader: Between the Blinds*, ed. P. Kamuf (New York: Columbia University Press, 1991), 255.

39. Derrida, "Living On: Borderlines," 95.

40. Ibid., 80.

41. Ibid., 121.

42. Ibid., 135.

43. Ibid., 108.

44. Lyotard, "The Survivor," 144.

45. Des Pres, *The Survivor*, 104.

46. Derrida, "Living On: Borderlines," 125.

47. Ibid., 76.

48. Ibid., 77.

49. Ibid., 87.

50. Ibid., 81–101.

51. See Jacques Derrida, *Dissemination*, trans. B. Johnson (Chicago: University of Chicago Press, 1981), 1–59.

52. Derrida, "Living On: Borderlines," 82.

53. Ibid., 81.

54. Ibid., 82.

55. Ibid., 95.

56. Ibid., 107.

57. Ibid., 146.

58. Ibid., 84.

59. On this caveat to theories of intertextuality, see Timothy K. Beal, "Ideology and Intertextuality: Surplus of Meaning and Controlling the Means of Production," in *Reading between Texts: Intertextuality and the Hebrew Bible*, ed. Danna Nolan Fewell (Louisville: Westminster/John Knox Press, 1992), 28.

60. Derrida, "Living On: Borderlines," 142.

61. Ibid., 144.

62. Theodor Adorno, *Negative Dialectics*, trans. E. B. Ashton (New York: Continuum, 1973), 65. Admittedly, I am taking Adorno's phrase out of context, but

not I think out of the spirit in which it was intended. The full quote would read: "The ontological need would no more guarantee its object than the agony of the starving assures them of food."

Chapter Two

1. Hermann Gunkel and Joachim Begrich, *Einleitung in die Psalmen: Die Gattungen der religiösen Lyrik Israels* (Göttingen: Vandenhoeck & Ruprecht, 1933), 136.

2. The two examples of dirges over the death of individuals most often cited are David's elegies for Saul and Jonathan (2 Sam. 1:19–27) and for Abner (2 Sam. 3:33–34). Examples of the dirge form being used as an anticipatory oracle of the fate of a nation are found in the prophets (e.g., Amos 5:2; Ezek. 27:2–11; Isa. 14:4–21). On the "genre" (*Gattung*) of the dirge, see esp. Hedwig Jahnow, *Das hebräische Leichenlied*, 124-62; Otto Eissfeldt, *The Old Testament: An Introduction*, trans. Peter Ackroyd (New York: Harper and Row, 1965), 94–98; and Westermann, *Lamentations*, 1–9.

3. Jahnow, *Das hebräische Leichenlied*, 170–71.

4. Ibid., 170.

5. Gunkel and Begrich, *Einleitung in die Psalmen*, 397–403.

6. Eissfeldt, *The Old Testament*, 501–2.

7. Westermann, *Lamentations*, 118.

8. Ibid., 148.

9. See Provan, *Lamentations*, 34; Robin B. Salters, *Jonah and Lamentations* (Sheffield: JSOT Press, 1994), 102–3.

10. Gottwald, *Studies*, 37.

11. See Eissfeldt, *The Old Testament*, 501–2; Westermann, *Lamentations*, 117; Salters, *Jonah and Lamentations*, 102–3.

12. While I speak of the interchange between the voice of Zion and the voice of the "poet," I am aware that these are alternating literary personae within the poetry, both of which are obviously attributable to the poet-as-author. See W. Lanahan, "The Speaking Voice in the Book of Lamentations," *Journal of Biblical Literature* 93 (1974): 41–49, for an insistence on maintaining this distinction. It is conventional for scholars to refer to the narrative voice as that of the poet, however, a convention that I find useful to retain, especially given the fact that this persona calls attention in 2:13 to the poetic task in which it is involved.

13. Claus Westermann, *Praise and Lament in the Psalms* (Richmond: John Knox Press, 1981), 266.

14. The scribes who preserved the Hebrew texts of the Bible, in order to discourage the pronouncing of the holy proper name of Israel's God, preserved only the consonants y-h-w-h (known as the tetragrammaton), without the vowels necessary to pronounce the name. Following the convention of English translations, I will often render this proper name as "the LORD," though sometimes I will also simply transliterate the four letters as "YHWH."

15. Hillers (*Lamentations*, 88), citing a number of parallels in other ancient Near Eastern literature, writes that "this sale of members of the family is a stage preceding the final horror, cannibalism." This judgment is correct, but I think it

misses the deeper layer of foreshadowing in 1:11, that there is already a hint of cannibalism in the giving of the children for/as food.

16. On the form-critical designation "accusation against God" (*Anklage Gottes*), see Westermann, *Praise and Lament*, 176–77; Westermann, *Lamentations*, 91–93.

17. See Sigmund Freud, "Mourning and Melancholia," in *The Standard Edition of the Complete Psychological Works*, vol. 14, trans. James Strachey (London: Hogarth, 1954); Jacques Derrida, "By Force of Mourning," *Critical Inquiry* 22 (1996): 171–92. I will return to the distinction between mourning and melancholia in relation to the book of Lamentations in chapter seven.

18. I will consider more closely the content of 1:12–16 below. In the present section I am primarily concerned with the generic slippage it represents.

19. For example, the statement that Jerusalem has become "unclean" (נדה) may indicate the impurity associated with a corpse (cf. Numbers 19:11–20 for such a usage).

20. I am taking the Hebrew term כמות as an example of the asseverative *kaph*, which as Gordis (*The Song of Songs and Lamentations*, 159) points out was recognized by medieval Jewish commentators but largely ignored by moderns. On this reading the sense of כמות is not "like death," but "there is death."

21. For a discussion of these form-critical elements in laments, see esp. Westermann, *Lamentations*, 136–37; Ferris, *Genre of Communal Lament*, 136–47.

22. Jorge Semprun, *The Long Voyage*, trans. R. Seaver (London: Weidenfeld and Nicholson, 1963), 71.

23. Jean Améry, *At the Mind's Limit*, 68, 71 (emphasis in original).

24. Westermann, *Lamentations*, 148.

25. This mixture of life and death, of dirge and lament, is also present in the Mesopotamian city laments, in which the city is presented as destroyed and is the subject of a dirge, but in which the goddess of the city is presented as alive and the speaking subject of a lament in the hope of getting a response from the divine assembly. In the biblical book of Lamentations, however, the destroyed city and the lamenting goddess have been combined into one figure, thus more pointedly introducing the paradox of survival. On the Mesopotamian city laments and their relationship to Lamentations, see esp. Dobbs-Allsopp, *Weep, O Daughter of Zion*.

26. Des Pres, *The Survivor*, 42.

27. I leave out the initial Hebrew phrase of the verse, לוא אליכם, though I admit this is not a completely satisfactory solution to the perennial problem it has presented translators. Nevertheless, the words do represent an anacrusis, falling outside the 3:2 meter of the rest of the verse. Obviously they are an interjection, though whether originally directed by Zion to the passersby (and thus original to the text) or by an editor to the reader (and thus a gloss that has made its way into the text) seems finally undecidable.

28. The Masoretic text's נשקד על פשעי (*niśqad ʿōl pᵉšāʿay*) has proven very perplexing for commentators throughout the centuries. Hillers, *Lamentations*, 73, proposes emending the phrase slightly to read נשקד על פשעי (*niśqad ʿal pᵉšāʿay*), resulting in the statement that "watch is kept over my steps." The emendation

makes good sense in the context of 1:14, though the evidence he marshals for it is by no means definitive. It nevertheless points to the difficulty of reading the Masoretic text as it stands.

29. The figure of Zion refers to her children as שוממים, the sense of which is difficult to capture when applied to people (cf. 2 Sam. 13:20 and Isa. 54:1) rather than to land or cities (cf. Jer. 18:16 and Isa. 54:3). When applied to cities the term implies "desertion," and perhaps the connotation here is something like "my children are as if deserted" (i.e., because taken into exile away from their mother). That is probably narrowing the sense too much, however, and I have settled on "ravage," which carries a broader meaning and retains the terror of violence demanded by the context.

30. Hillers, Lamentations, 75.

31. Compare, e.g., 2 Kings 4:19, "my head, my head!" (ראשי ראשי), and Jer. 4:19, "my anguish, my anguish!" (מעי מעי). On the basis of these examples, it seems that Westermann (Lamentations, 113) is mistaken in his assertion that such doubling indicates emphasis "only in the case of verbal forms."

32. Des Pres, The Survivor, 44.

33. Westermann, Lamentations, 135–36 (emphasis in original).

34. Des Pres, The Survivor, 49.

35. On this aspect of the lament, see esp. Westermann, The Psalms: Structure, Content, and Message (Minneapolis: Fortress Press, 1980), 35–43; Westermann, Praise and Lament, 265–80; Patrick D. Miller, They Cried to the Lord: The Form and Theology of Biblical Prayer (Minneapolis: Fortress Press, 1994), 135–77.

36. Irving Greenberg, "Cloud of Smoke, Pillar of Fire: Judaism, Christianity, and Modernity after the Holocaust," in Auschwitz: Beginning of a New Era? ed. E. Fleischner (New York: Ktav, 1977), 23.

37. Elie Wiesel, A Jew Today (New York: Random House, 1978), 235.

38. Ibid.

39. Theodor Adorno, Prisms, trans. S. Weber (Cambridge: MIT Press, 1981), 30.

40. Adorno, Negative Dialectics, 362–63.

41. I take the mem of לבם as functioning adverbially, yielding the sense of "from the heart." So also Thomas F. McDaniel, "Philological Studies in Lamentations, II," Biblica 49 (1968): 203–4; Dobbs-Allsopp, Weep, O Daughter of Zion, 34.

42. The phrase is Westermann's, used repeatedly in his Lamentations, 127, 130, 140.

43. For summaries of this position, see Samuel Balentine, Prayer in the Hebrew Bible: The Drama of Divine-Human Dialogue (Minneapolis: Fortress Press, 1995), 148–50; Miller, They Cried to the Lord, 55–57.

44. Westermann, The Psalms, 29–51; Westermann, Praise and Lament, 52–64.

45. Westermann, Lamentations, 156.

46. Ibid., 157.

47. So, for example, in the standard Brown-Driver-Briggs Hebrew lexicon.

48. Wilhelm Rudolph, Die Klagelieder (Gütersloh: Gütersloher Verlagshaus Gerd Mohn, 1962), 258.

49. So Westermann, Lamentations, 210; following Max Löhr, Der Klagelieder des Jeremias (Göttingen: Vandenhoeck & Ruprecht, 1906), 31–32; and others.

50. So Hillers, Lamentations, 160; Provan, Lamentations, 133; and others.

51. Westermann, The Psalms, 42.

Chapter Three

1. Derrida, "Living On: Borderlines," 152.

2. Alan Mintz, Hurban: Responses to Catastrophe in Hebrew Literature (New York: Columbia University Press, 1984), 44.

3. Claus Westermann, Isaiah 40–66: A Commentary, Old Testament Library (Philadelphia: Westminster Press, 1969), 34.

4. Gottwald, Studies, 44–45; Max Löhr, "Der Sprachgebrauch des Buches der Klagelieder," Zeitschrift für die alttestamentliche Wissenschaft 14 (1894): 31–50.

5. Carol Newsom, "Response to Norman K. Gottwald, 'Social Class and Ideology in Isaiah 40–55,'" Semeia 58 (1992): 75.

6. Patricia Tull Willey, Remember the Former Things: The Recollection of Previous Texts in Second Isaiah, Society of Biblical Literature Dissertation Series 161 (Atlanta: Scholars Press, 1997).

7. Ibid., 1.

8. Ibid., 141.

9. Ibid., 1.

10. Ibid., 89.

11. See the useful chart on the distribution of names in Peter Wilcox and David Paton-Williams, "The Servant Songs in Deutero-Isaiah," Journal for the Study of the Old Testament 42 (1988): 82, though I disagree with their final analysis in many ways. It is possible that Zion and Jerusalem are addressed in the "prologue" in 40:9, though here it is not clear if one is to understand Zion/Jerusalem as the "herald" or as the one addressed by the herald.

12. S. R. Driver, An Introduction to the Literature of the Old Testament, 9th ed. (Edinburgh: T. & T. Clark, 1913), 231.

13. I do not take the statement that "Judah is exiled" in Lamentations 1:3 as referring to the city of Zion, contra Newsom, "Response," 76; and Saul M. Olyan, "Honor, Shame, and Covenant Relations in Ancient Israel and Its Environment," Journal of Biblical Literature 115 (1996): 215, but rather to the nation of Judah. This helps to explain the very problematic grammatical construction immediately following, מעני ומרב עבדה, which many scholars and versions have tried to explain in a causative sense, i.e., "because of suffering and much toil." As Hillers argues, this is a very strained reading. But one need not resort to his explanation that the mem particle here implies a temporal sense, i.e., "after suffering and much toil" (Hillers, Lamentations, 66). Also unnecessary is the suggestion by Robert Gordis (The Song of Songs and Lamentations, 153) of a "Mem of condition," thereby producing the translation "in poverty and oppression." Rather, the plain sense of the mem particle can be retained by taking Judah as the people who have gone into exile "from suffering and much toil," namely, the situation in Jerusalem. Likewise, the reference in 1:7 to Jerusalem's ימי עניה ומרודיה

need not be taken as meaning "exile." The phrase ‏עניה ומרודיה‎ is likely a hendiadys indicating the "wandering poor" or "beggars" (for such a usage, see Isa. 58:7).

14. Excepting the opening proclamation of 40:1–11, which may be construed as an opening to Second Isaiah in its entirety and thus not really a part of the section that I refer to as "chapters 40–48."

15. The following chart is taken from Willey, *Remember the Former Things,* 105–6.

16. This section is addressed to a second-person masculine plural audience that, as Willey writes, "seems to correspond most closely to the prophet's actual audience" (ibid., 180).

17. Ibid., 221–26.

18. Contra, e.g., Leland Wilshire, "Jerusalem as the 'Servant-City' in Isaiah 40–66: Reflections in the Light of Further Study of the Cuneiform Tradition," in *The Bible in the Light of Cuneiform Literature,* ed. W. W. Hallo, B. W. Jones, and G. L. Mattingly (Lewiston: Edwin Mellen Press, 1990); Christopher Seitz, *Zion's Final Destiny: The Development of the Book of Isaiah* (Minneapolis: Fortress Press, 1995), 202–5.

19. See esp. T. N. D. Mettinger, *A Farewell to the Servant Songs: A Critical Examination of an Exegetical Axiom* (Lund: CWK Gleerup, 1983); Wilcox and Paton-Williams, "The Servant Songs"; J. F. A. Sawyer, "Daughter of Zion and Servant of the Lord in Isaiah: A Comparison," *Journal for the Study of the Old Testament* 44 (1989): 89–107.

20. So Mettinger, *Farewell to the Servant Songs,* 35; Willey, *Remember the Former Things,* 191.

21. Wilcox and Paton-Williams, "The Servant Songs," 80.

22. This is pointed out by Wilshire, "Jerusalem as the 'Servant-City,'" 357: "One should not go beyond the text and seek throughout history for a 'Servant of the Lord' any more than one should seek for an historical manifestation of a 'virgin daughter' or a 'barren wife,' other basic images used by Deutero-Isaiah."

23. Willey, *Remember the Former Things,* 232–33.

24. See Tod Linafelt, "Surviving Lamentations," *Horizons in Biblical Theology* 17 (1995): 56; reprinted in *A Feminist Companion to Reading the Bible,* ed. A. Brenner and C. Fontaine (Sheffield: Sheffield Academic Press, 1997). This was first suggested to me by Walter Brueggemann in a private conversation. I found later that Norman Gottwald (*Studies,* 44) lists it among the verbal correspondences between Lamentations and Second Isaiah, though he does not treat it. See also Willey, *Remember the Former Things,* 189–93. Benjamin D. Sommer, *A Prophet Reads Scripture: Allusion in Isaiah 40–66* (Stanford: Stanford University Press, 1998), undertakes a comprehensive study, similar to Willey's, of Second Isaiah's use of other biblical texts. His treatment of Lamentations is, however, very brief (127–30) and makes no mention of the allusion to Lamentations 5:20 in Isaiah 49.

25. As noted also by Willey, *Remember the Former Things,* 189. The three other occurrences of the word pair may be found in Isa. 65:11, Prov. 2:17, and Job 9:27.

26. Walter Benjamin, "The Work of Art in the Age of Mechanical Reproduction," in *Illuminations,* trans. H. Zohn (New York: Schocken Books, 1968), 214.

27. Ibid., 215.

28. For this translation of the Hebrew כי אם-מאס מאסתנו קצפת עלינו עד-מאד, see my discussion in chapter two above.

29. Derrida, "Living On: Borderlines," 147.

30. Willey, *Remember the Former Things*, 188–92.

31. Jan Kochanowski, *Laments* [*Treny*], trans. S. Baranzcak and S. Heaney (New York: Farrar, Straus and Giroux, 1995), 21.

32. Lyotard, "The Survivor," 151.

33. Ibid.

34. Derrida, "Living On: Borderlines," 77.

35. Ibid., 76.

36. My translation of verse 21 leaves out the phrase "exiled and lost" (גלה וסורה), as suggested by the critical apparatus in *Biblia Hebraica Stuttgartensia*. It is not clear to whom this phrase refers, since Zion is not portrayed in Second Isaiah as exiled but rather as abandoned in Judah. Without the phrase, the verse is nicely parallel.

37. I emend the Hebrew צדיק here to עריץ, with 1QIsᵃ, the Syriac, and the Vulgate.

38. Benjamin, "The Work of Art," 230.

39. Willey, *Remember the Former Things*, 223–24.

Chapter Four

1. Benjamin, "Task of the Translator," 72.

2. Derrida, "Living On: Borderlines," 84.

3. See my treatment in chapter two of the poet's use of the keyword "pouring out" (שפך) in the book of Lamentations.

4. Benjamin, "Aufgabe des Übersetzers," 10.

5. Derrida, "Living On: Borderlines," 134.

6. Meyer Waxman, *A History of Jewish Literature*, vol. 1 (New York: Bloch, 1930), 112.

7. On the rabbinic rules governing targum, see Avigdor Shinan, "Live Translation: On the Nature of the Aramaic Targums to the Pentateuch," *Prooftexts* 3 (1983): 41–49; and Philip S. Alexander, "The Targumim and the Rabbinic Rules for the Delivery of the Targum," in *Vetus Testamentum Supplement* 36 (*Salamanca Congress Volume*), ed. J. A. Emerton (Leiden: E. J. Brill, 1985).

8. Alexander Samely, *The Interpretation of Speech in the Pentateuch Targums* (Tübingen: J. C. B. Mohr, 1992), 158.

9. Ibid.

10. Samely (ibid., 160–62) makes this feature of targum very clear by comparing Pseudo-Jonathan's rendering of Genesis 12:10–13 with the *Genesis Apocryphon* XIX, 10–20. The targum builds around the Hebrew narrative, leaving it essentially intact, while the *Genesis Apocryphon* completely rewrites the narrative, retaining little of the original Hebrew wording or sequence and even changing the point of view from third to first person, something the targum would never do.

11. John Bowker, "Haggadah in the Targum Onkelos," *Journal of Semitic Studies* 12 (1967): 13.

12. Alexander Sperber, *The Bible in Aramaic*, vol. 4B, *The Targum and the Hebrew Bible* (Leiden: E. J. Brill, 1973), 21.

13. Waxman, *History of Jewish Literature*, 1:118.

14. Ibid.

15. Etan Levine, *The Aramaic Version of Lamentations* (New York: Sepher-Hermon Press, 1976), 14.

16. Samely, *Interpretation of Speech*, 181.

17. Benjamin, "Aufgabe des Übersetzers," 12.

18. Benjamin, "Task of the Translator," 71.

19. Ibid.

20. Shinan, "Live Translation," 44.

21. Jacques Derrida, "Des Tours de Babel," *Semeia* 54 (1991): 20.

22. Ibid.

23. Philip Alexander, "The Textual Tradition of Targum Lamentations," *Abr-Nahrain* 24 (1986): 2, however, has urged caution in fixing too certainly the provenance of Targum Lamentations, noting that while it contains some Greek loan words and much Palestinian Aramaic, thereby indicating a Western origin, it also contains Onqelos-type Aramaic and certain words otherwise unattested in Palestinian Aramaic. And while Maimonides and other medieval scholars referred to Targum Lamentations as "Targum Yerushalmi," there is also a medieval tradition that at least some of the targumim to the Writings originated with the Babylonian scholar Rav Joseph.

24. Albert van der Heide, *The Yemenite Tradition of the Targum of Lamentations* (Leiden: E. J. Brill, 1981), 35; Alexander, "Textual Tradition," 8–9.

25. Alexander, "Textual Tradition," 7.

26. Of the two, van der Heide's is the superior. Though basing his edition on the Yemenite Text, Sperber (*Bible in Aramaic*, vol. 4A) imports expansions from the Western Text, thereby conflating the two distinct recensions. He also makes numerous mistakes in copying the British Library manuscript Or 2375, which are identified in appendix 2 of van der Heide, *Yemenite Tradition*, 53–55.

27. Most egregious is his identification of an Esther Scroll, "Salonika, University I (1532)," as a Lamentations manuscript. As van der Heide (*Yemenite Tradition*, 58) first deduced, the siglum "S" in Levine's original papers must have stood for "Sperber," since the variants he lists as deriving from the Salonika manuscript (under the siglum "S") in fact reproduce Sperber's 1968 edition of the Yemenite Text. See also Alexander, "Textual Tradition," 6.

28. Alexander, "Textual Tradition," 10.

29. See the article by Christian M. M. Brady, "Targum Lamentations 1:1–4: A Theological Prologue," forthcoming in *Targumic Studies*, vol. 3. I am grateful to the author for providing a prepublication version of this article.

30. See Louis Ginzberg, *The Legends of the Jews*, vol. 6 (Philadelphia: Jewish Publication Society, 1968), 96, for the midrashic reference.

31. Levine, *The Aramaic Version of Lamentations*, 20.

32. Westermann, *Lamentations*, 135.

33. Translations from Targum Lamentations in this chapter are my own, based on Etan Levine's edition of the Western Text, though on occasion I will make reference to Albert van der Heide's edition of the Yemenite Text. All emphases are mine and serve to highlight the targumic expansions to the biblical text.

34. Interestingly, while deleting the second repetition of "my eye," the targum replaces it with the phrase "like a spring of water," thereby maintaining the intensifying quality of the repetition.

35. Actually, the Hebrew word for "my life" (נפשי), present in the second italicized addition, is also present in biblical Lamentations as the object of the verb "to restore" (משיב). In the Western recension of Targum Lamentations it is separated from the lexical equivalent of the verb משיב, and recontextualized as the object of a second verbal phrase missing from the biblical text.

36. The Yemenite recension refers to "women" (נשיא) rather than "the daughters of Israel" (בנאתא דישראל), and it lacks the qualification "from starvation" (בכפנא).

37. The Attribute of Justice is in rabbinic thought a quality of God, though it sometimes is personified as though it were distinct from God, as happens here in Targum Lamentations. Elsewhere it is even portrayed as addressing God (b. Shabbat 55a). The Attribute of Justice is often presented in relation to the Attribute of Mercy (מדת רחמים). According to a midrash in Bereshit Rabbah (12:15), both attributes were involved in the creation of the world; had either been missing, the world could not have endured. A very interesting variant occurs in a group of Yemenite manuscripts of Targum Lamentations, which substitute "the Attribute of Mercy" (מדת רחמין) for the Attribute of Justice in this passage.

38. The avenging of the death of Zechariah is a popular midrashic motif. Variations on it can be found in Eikhah Rabbah II, 23, and the Talmud (b. Yoma 38b). In the New Testament (Matt. 23:35; Luke 11:51) Jesus makes similar use of the figure of Zechariah.

39. It should be noted that the final line of 2:22 in Targum Lamentations, though not a major supplement, expands the final line of the biblical text by adding a prepositional phrase to each verb. Thus, the phrase "those I clasped/dandled" (טפח) becomes the targum's "those I clasped/wrapped (לפף) in linen," and "those I raised up" becomes "those I raised up on regal dainties." The additions serve to emphasize the care with which the children were treated previously, and to contrast more starkly with their present fate.

40. Cited in Levine, The Aramaic Version of Lamentations, 15.

41. Ibid., 121.

42. Derrida, "Des Tours de Babel," 20.

43. This is similar to the understanding of midrash offered by Daniel Boyarin, Intertextuality and the Reading of Midrash (Bloomington: Indiana University Press, 1991), 15, in which "[t]he dialogue and dialectic of the midrashic rabbis [are] understood as readings of the dialogue and dialectic of the biblical text."

44. Derrida writes here about a "complement" in similar terms that he uses

for his notion of "supplement" elsewhere. See esp. Jacques Derrida, *Of Grammatology*, trans. G. Spivak (Baltimore: Johns Hopkins University Press, 1974), 313.

45. Robert Detweiler, "Overliving," *Semeia* 54 (1991): 240.

46. Note too that the reference to restoration in Ezekiel 34 is spoken by YHWH in the first person, but as it is brought into the targum it is transformed into the speech of Zion.

47. Benjamin, "Task of the Translator," 78.

48. De Man, *The Resistance to Theory*, 92.

49. Etan Levine, *The Aramaic Version of the Bible: Contents and Contexts* (New York: Walter de Gruyter, 1988), 174.

50. Ibid., 178.

51. Ibid.

52. The idea of punishment is well represented in the opening verses of Targum Lamentations, which offer explanations for the destruction based on the history of Israel's disobedience to YHWH. But this in no way lessens the later passages that do not fit into this notion of retribution. The expansions in these opening verses do not have to be read as setting the tone for how the entire targum is to be read (so Brady, "Targum Lamentations 1:1–4"). Rather they reflect the tone of the opening verses of the Masoretic text of Lamentations, which does not hold sway for the entire book.

52. Shinan, "Live Translation," 46.

53. Ibid., 47.

Chapter Five

1. Geoffrey Hartman, "The Struggle for the Text," in *Midrash and Literature*, ed. G. Hartman and S. Budick (New Haven: Yale University Press, 1986), 9.

2. Michael Fishbane, *The Garments of Torah: Essays in Biblical Hermeneutics* (Bloomington: Indiana University Press, 1989), 37.

3. Introduction to *Zion in Jewish Literature*, ed. Abraham S. Halkin (New York: Herzl Press, 1961), 1.

4. On the continuing hope of Palestinian Jews for the rebuilding of the temple after 70 C.E., see Gerson D. Cohen, "Zion in Rabbinic Literature," in *Zion in Jewish Literature*, ed. A. Halkin, 56; Shaye J. D. Cohen, "The Destruction: From Scripture to Midrash," *Prooftexts* 2 (1982): 18; and H. L. Strack and G. Stemberger, *Introduction to the Talmud and Midrash* (Minneapolis: Fortress Press, 1992), 5.

5. James Kugel, "Two Introductions to Midrash," in *Midrash and Literature*, ed. G. Hartman and S. Budick (New Haven: Yale University Press, 1986), 72.

6. Menahem Mendel Kasher, *Torah Shelemah* [Hebrew], vol. 1 (Jerusalem: n.p., 5687/1927). See also the abridged English translation, *Encyclopedia of Biblical Interpretation: A Millennial Anthology*, vol. 1, trans. Harry Freedman (New York: American Biblical Encyclopedia Society, 1953), which devotes twenty-eight pages to this single verse.

7. Detweiler, "Overliving," 243.

8. Maimonides, *The Guide of the Perplexed*, trans. S. Pines (Chicago: University of Chicago Press, 1963), III:43.

9. Max Kadushin, *The Rabbinic Mind* (New York: Bloch, 1952), 132.

10. See esp. Barry Holtz, "Midrash," in *Back to the Sources*, ed. B. Holtz (New York: Summit, 1984); David Stern, "Midrash and the Language of Exegesis," in *Midrash and Literature*, ed. G. Hartman and S. Budick (New Haven: Yale University Press, 1986); Daniel Boyarin, *Intertextuality and the Reading of Midrash*.

11. Holtz, "Midrash," 180; Boyarin, *Intertextuality and the Reading of Midrash*, 14.

12. Alan Mintz, *Hurban*, 57–62; David Stern, "Imitatio Hominis: Anthropomorphism and the Character(s) of God in Rabbinic Literature," *Prooftexts* 12 (1992): 151–74; and David Kraemer, *Responses to Suffering in Classical Rabbinic Literature* (Oxford: Oxford University Press, 1995), 140–46.

13. The section under consideration can be found in S. Buber, *Midrasch Echa Rabbati* (Vilnius: Druck und Verlag von Wittwe und Gebruder Romm, 1899), 25–28. The translations from the Hebrew in this chapter are my own and are made from Buber's text, which represents the Ashkenazic recension. There exists a Sephardic recension as well, but currently there is no critical text of it, on which see David Stern, *Parables in Midrash: Narrative and Exegesis in Rabbinic Literature* (Cambridge: Harvard University Press, 1991), 245–50. Like all who have worked on Eikhah Rabbah, I have often consulted Cohen's translation for the Soncino edition of *Midrash Rabbah*, ed. H. Freedman and M. Simon (London: Soncino Press, 1939) and have benefited greatly from it. Other useful translations into English include Jacob Neusner, *Lamentations Rabbah: An Analytical Translation* (Atlanta: Scholars Press, 1989), and D. Stern and M. Mirsky, *Rabbinic Fantasies* (Philadelphia: Jewish Publication Society, 1990).

14. Stern, "Imitatio Hominis," 158.

15. Ibid., 159.

16. Neusner sees this section (i.e., the story of the patriarchs approaching God to mourn the fate of Israel) as an independent unit, thus making for three stories rather than two, although he admits that he "cannot make a strong case for my division" (*Lamentations Rabbah*, 79). Stern posits only two stories, which have been combined at some point in transmission, the second beginning with Samuel bar Nahman's story below. In either case, both agree the final form is a legitimate object of interpretation in its own right.

17. Stern, "Imitatio Hominis," 160.

18. Ibid., 161.

19. Cohen, "The Destruction," 34.

20. Buber, *Midrasch Echa Rabbati*, 26–28.

21. Stern, "Imitatio Hominis," 162.

22. How best to translate this verse is a matter of much debate among scholars of Lamentations. (See my treatment of 5:22 in chapter two.) It is not at all clear that a question is implied by the opening phrase כי אם, though I have rendered it as such here in order to bring out the parallel with Jeremiah 14:19. The parallel is based less on the status of Lamentations 5:22 as a question than it is on the parallel use of the infinitive construct of מאס ("reject").

23. Stern, "Midrash and the Language of Exegesis," 108.

24. On the terms "infrastructure" and "superstructure" as they relate to midrashic exegesis, see ibid., 111.

25. For a history of the legend of Abraham carrying out the sacrifice of Isaac, see Solomon Spiegel, *The Last Trial* (New York: Schocken Books, 1969).

26. Elsewhere in Eikhah Rabbah, the connection between the acrostic structure of Lamentations and the extent of Israel's transgressing is made explicit. For example, in a comment on Lamentations 1:1 it is said that the acrostic form of the poetry represents the complete transgression of the Torah from א to ת (that is, from the first to the last letter of the Hebrew alphabet).

27. Stern, "Imitatio Hominis," 162.

28. Kraemer, *Responses to Suffering*, 144.

29. Ibid., 145.

30. Neusner, *Lamentations Rabbah*, 78.

31. Kraemer, *Responses to Suffering*, 145.

32. Stern, "Imitatio Hominis," 163.

33. Ibid., 164.

34. Mintz, *Hurban*, 62.

35. Emil Fackenheim, *To Mend the World: Foundations of Post-Holocaust Jewish Thought* (New York: Schocken Books, 1989), 252.

Chapter Six

1. Martin Heidegger, *Poetry, Language, Thought*, trans. A. Hofstadter (New York: Harper and Row, 1971), 91.

2. Seamus Heaney, *The Redress of Poetry* (New York: Farrar, Straus, and Giroux, 1995), 4.

3. For a summary of the views concerning the dating of the *payyetanim*, see Ismar Elbogen, *Jewish Liturgy: A Comprehensive History*, trans. R. Scheindlin (Philadelphia: Jewish Publication Society, 1993), 244; Jacob J. Petuchowski, *Theology and Poetry: Studies in the Medieval Piyyut* (London: Routledge and Kegan Paul, 1978), 13–14.

4. Petuchowski, *Theology and Poetry*, 4.

5. Maimonides, *The Guide*, I, 59.

6. Ibid.

7. Cited in Petuchowski, *Theology and Poetry*, 6.

8. Elbogen (*Jewish Liturgy*, 245) writes: "He was the lawgiver of the *piyyut* for subsequent generations and served as a model for later poets."

9. Translations from the Hebrew texts of the *kinot* in this chapter are my own, though I have found it useful to consult the translations of the first and second poem in *The Penguin Book of Hebrew Verse*, ed. and trans. T. Carmi (New York: Penguin Books, 1981); and the translations of the second and third poem in *The Authorized Kinot for the Ninth of Av*, trans. Abraham Rosenfeld (London: Labworth and Co., 5725/1965). For the complete Hebrew texts of the *kinot*, along with my rather literal English translations, see the appendix below.

10. The idea that there is a "definite structure" to experiences of survival is

from Des Pres, *The Survivor*, v. In response to this idea, Langer emphasized the different "versions of survival" (*Versions of Survival*, xi). But the two positions are not mutually exclusive, especially when applied to the survival of literature as I am doing here.

11. In fact, Ted Carmi's title for the poem is "The Dialogue of Zion and God" (*The Penguin Book of Hebrew Poetry*, 223).

12. It is possible, as David Blumenthal points out to me, that an indirect address to God is implied here (see Psalm 145 for an example of such address). Even if not intended as indirect address, the woman's speech certainly functions that way, as the response that follows it demonstrates.

13. For the text of this poem, see Carmi, *Penguin Book of Hebrew Poetry*, 221.

14. I am grateful to Michael Koplow for suggesting the phrase "Can it be true?" This rendering picks up on the fact that, as traditional commentatiors on Kallir have noted, the first three letters of each line of the poem—א, מ (the word-final form of which is ם), and ת—spell out the Hebrew word for "truth." In my translation of this poem in the appendix I use the phrase for the first four lines, and then occasionally after that, but technically it would be more accurate to use it as an opening for every line.

15. I call attention to the fact once again that the theme of cannibalism in these texts is strictly a literary motif; that is, one should take it neither as a description of what actually happened in the siege of Jerusalem nor of what Kallir thinks happened.

16. It is possible too that Kallir alludes to the "children of your bereavement" (בני שכליך) from Isaiah 49:20, but reverses the more positive treatment in Second Isaiah to fit the unrelenting tone of the *kinah*.

17. See the treatment of this text by Deborah Krause, "A Blessing Cursed: The Prophet's Prayer for Barren Womb and Dry Breasts in Hosea 9," in *Reading between Texts: Intertextuality and the Hebrew Bible*, ed. D. N. Fewell (Louisville: Westminster/ John Knox Press, 1992).

18. The combination of an Aramaic word with a Hebrew plural ending would not be beyond the bounds of the *payyetanim*, who regularly stretch the rules of grammar and create neologisms at will.

19. Kallir is known for making intentional use of midrash as a source for his piyyutim, perhaps the first liturgical poet to do so. See Leopold Zunz, *Literaturgeschichte der synagogalen Poesie* (Berlin: L. Gerschel, 1865), 29, on this aspect of Kallir's poems.

20. For the complete text of the story in 4 Ezra, see *The Old Testament Pseudepigrapha*, ed. James H. Charlesworth (Garden City, N.Y.: Doubleday, 1983), 545–48.

21. Though Kallir knew and used the messianic and apocalyptic writings that were available to him (so Zunz, *Literaturgeschichte*, 603), it is unlikely that he knew the story from 4 Ezra, which was not preserved in rabbinic sources but rather in translation in Christian communities.

22. On the character and practices of Tisha b'Av, see A. Z. Idelsohn, *Jewish*

Liturgy and Its Development (New York: Henry Holt, 1932), 253–56; or Abraham Millgram, *Jewish Worship* (Philadelphia: Jewish Publication Society, 1971), 276–83.

23. Benjamin, "Task of the Translator," 72.

24. For more on the argument that the month of Tishri, which Rosh Hashanah begins, should be considered as the beginning point of the year rather than Nisan, see Arthur Waskow, *Seasons of Our Joy: A Modern Guide to the Jewish Holidays* (Boston: Beacon Press, 1982), 1–21.

Chapter Seven

1. David G. Roskies, *Against the Apocalypse: Responses to Catastrophe in Modern Jewish Culture* (Cambridge: Harvard University Press, 1984), 11.

2. Ibid., 22.

3. Introduction to *Truth and Lamentation: Stories and Poems on the Holocaust*, ed. Milton Teichman and Sharon Leder (Urbana: University of Illinois Press, 1994), 19. The title of another recent anthology of poetry on the Holocaust, *Beyond Lament: Poets of the World Bearing Witness to the Holocaust*, ed. Marguerite M. Striar (Evanston, Ill: Northwestern University Press, 1998), implies a similar need to move beyond what is seen as the traditional response to suffering.

4. For more on reading Edmond Jabès in relation to the book of Lamentations, see Tod Linafelt, "Margins of Lamentation, or, The Unbearable Whiteness of Reading," in *Reading Bibles, Writing Bodies: Identity and the Book*, ed. Timothy K. Beal and David M. Gunn (London and New York: Routledge Press, 1997). On the work of Jabès more generally, see esp. Matthew Del Nevo, "Reading Edmond Jabès," *Literature and Theology* 9 (1995): 399–422.

5. Mintz, *Hurban*, 43.

6. "The Shawl" was first published in *The New Yorker* in 1980. It was reprinted, along with the novella "Rosa," in Cynthia Ozick, *The Shawl: A Story and Novella* (New York: Alfred A. Knopf, 1989), from which all quotes in the present chapter are drawn. The story has also been anthologized numerous times, most recently in *The Best American Short Stories of the Century*, ed. John Updike and Katrina Kenison (New York: Houghton Mifflin Co., 1999).

7. See the interview with Ozick in Joshua O. Haberman, *The God I Believe In* (New York: The Free Press, 1994), 153–73.

8. Ozick, "The Shawl," 5–6.

9. Ibid., 6.

10. Ibid., 8.

11. Ibid., 9.

12. Ibid., 9–10.

13. Ibid., 5.

14. Ibid., 8–10.

15. Ibid., 7.

16. Ibid., 5.

17. Ibid.

18. Sigmund Freud, "Mourning and Melancholia," 243. See also my treat-

ment of this theme in "The Impossibility of Mourning," in *God in the Fray: A Tribute to Walter Brueggemann*, ed. Tod Linafelt and Timothy K. Beal (Minneapolis: Fortress Press, 1998), from which some of the material in the present chapter is reprinted.

19. Freud, "Mourning and Melancholia," 244.

20. Ibid., 245.

21. Jacques Derrida, "By Force of Mourning," 177.

22. Ibid., 173.

23. Elaine Kauvar, *Cynthia Ozick's Fiction* (Bloomington: Indiana University Press, 1993), 182.

24. Naomi Seidman, "Burning the Book of Lamentations," in *Out of the Garden: Women Writers on the Bible*, ed. Christina Büchmann and Celina Spiegel (New York: Fawcett Columbine, 1994), 281.

Index

Abraham, 109–12
Adenay, Walter, 7–8
Adorno, Theodor, 1, 2, 14, 54, 155–56n. 62
afflict, use of term, 57
afterlife
  consolation and restoration in, 133–36
  guarantee absent for, 34
  participation in, 81–82
  stages in, 130
  translation as, 27–29, 86–87
  of work of art, 26–27, 80
  See also kinot; survival
Alexander, Philip, 88, 162n. 23
Améry, Jean, 21, 23–25, 41
Amichai, Yehuda, 134
anger, expression of, 59
Aramaic, translation to, 82–83
arena, as key word, 139–40
art
  reproduction of, 73, 80
  task of, 78, 86
  translatability and, 26–29
atomic bomb, survival of, 22–23
atrocities
  literary works linked to, 4
  survival juxtaposed to, 23
  survivor guilt and, 47–48
  See also Holocaust

Attribute of Justice
  concept of, 163n. 37
  focus of, 97
  targum on, 92–93
  Zion compared to, 95–96
Attribute of Mercy, 163n. 37

Babylon. See exiles (in Babylon)
Bar Kochba rebellion, 102
Baudelaire, Charles-Pierre, 25
Bauer, Yehudah, 153–54n. 12
Beal, Timothy K., 155
Begrich, Joachim, 36
Benjamin, Walter
  Derrida on, 29, 31, 94
  on reproduction of art, 73, 80
  on task of art, 78, 86
  on translation, 25–29, 34, 81, 82, 84, 86–87, 97
Betar, fall of, 131
Bettelheim, Bruno, 23, 24, 25
Bible
  as center of religion, 102–3
  diminished references to, 134–35
  opening gaps of, 104
  translation of, 82–83
  See also specific books
Bishop, Elizabeth, 4
Blanchot, Maurice, 30–31, 33, 74, 81
Bloom, Harold, 29

Blumenthal, David, 167n. 12
bosom/shawl, Lamentations and "Shawl" linked by, 139–40
Boyarin, Daniel, 163n. 43
Brandscheidt, Renate, 9–10, 12, 151n. 4
breaking of vessels, 28–29, 155n. 36
Brueggemann, Walter, 160n. 24
Buber, S., 165n. 13

cannibalism
  of enemies, 76, 78, 93
  as feast, 58
  foreshadowing of, 156–57n. 15
  kinot on, 122–25
  as literary motif, 167n. 15
  "Shawl" and Lamentations linked by, 140–41
  targum on, 92–93, 95–96
Carmi, Ted, 167n. 11
children of Zion
  concern for survival of, 18, 20, 56, 91–94, 107–8
  death sentence for, 33
  in defense of Israel, 112
  Eikhah Rabbah on, 105–15
  God's weeping for, 104–8, 110–11
  kinot on, 119
  pain of loss of, 46
  persuasive rhetoric concerned with, 50–58
  place of death for, 139–40
  as precious things, 40, 156–57n. 15
  as "ravaged," 76, 158n. 29
  restoration of, 73, 74–79, 80, 95–97, 108–15, 129–30
  suffering of, 14–15, 105–15, 123–26
  as symbols, 20, 72, 76–79
  Targum Lamentations on, 87, 89–97
  See also exiles (in Babylon); "The Shawl" (Ozick)
Childs, Brevard, 151n. 4
Christian bias, in interpretation, 5, 7–9, 69
Christian Church, lament language in, 13–14

Churgin, Pinkhos, 94
city-lament genre, 16–17, 157n. 25
Cohen, Shaye, 108, 165n. 13
comfort
  absence of, 55–56, 74, 138–39
  for exiles, 74–75
  Isaiah's call for, 64
  poet figure as, 53–54
  refusal to accept, 126–29
  refusal to give, 96
  speech linked to, 91
communal lament (genre)
  God's nonresponse to, 62
  God's response to, 73–74
  Lamentations 1 and 2 as, 37, 42
  Lamentations 5 as, 59–60
community, recovery of
  integration of exiles and, 63, 64, 67–68, 71–72
  suffering man as model of, 12
  survival and, 100–101
confrontation
  lament's forcing of, 13–14
  reconciliation favored over, 5, 9–13, 15
cult, ironic use of language of, 58
Cyrus, 66

Daniel, 111
David, 95, 156n. 2
Davidson, Israel, 119
death
  of author, 19–20, 21, 30
  excessive, 63
  life in midst of, 35–43, 136
  memory of, 20–21
  romantic notions of, 24–25
  triumph of life and, 32–34
deconstruction, text's borders in, 32–34
Delbo, Charlotte, 23, 25
de Man, Paul, 26, 29
Derrida, Jacques
  on complement/supplement, 163–64n. 44
  on mourning, 142–43
  on survival of texts, 19–20, 29–34, 63

on Lamentations, 3–4, 88–89, 103
motifs in, 163n. 38
on Second Isaiah, 63–64
survival via, 101–4
targum and, 84–85, 103
task of, 100–101
See also Eikhah Rabbah; Targum Lamentations
Miller, J. Hillis, 29
Mintz, Alan
on Rachel, 115
on Second Isaiah, 135–36
on suffering man, 6–7, 12
Mirsky, M., 165n. 13
Mishnah, 83
Moses
God as judge and, 108
God reproached by, 114
God's weeping and, 106–7
Israel defended by, 111–13
mother, Rachel as, 109, 114–15
See also children of Zion; Zion figure
mourning
of God, 104–8, 110–11
impossibility of, 142–43
melancholia compared to, 40–41, 141–42
See also grief
mutation, translation as, 86–87
mysticism, translatability and, 28–29

Nahman, Samuel bar, 108, 165n. 16
Neusner, Jacob, 114, 165n. 13, 165n. 16
Newsom, Carol, 64–65, 67, 73, 159–60n. 13
New Yorker, Ozick's "Shawl" in, 168n. 6
Numbers, 89, 112

O'Connor, Kathleen M., 151n. 4
Olson, Eric, 24, 25
Olyan, Saul M., 159–60n. 13
onein, God as, 107–8
Ozick, Cynthia, 136
See also "The Shawl" (Ozick)

Pagis, Dan, 134
pain, expression of, 43–49
See also suffering, expression of
Paton-Williams, David, 66, 159n. 11
persuasion rhetoric
in Eikhah Rabbah, 104–5
in Lamentations, 49–58
in Second Isaiah, 66–67
Peshitta, 60
pity, as key word, 138–39
piyyutim. See kinot; medieval Hebrew poetry
Plöger, Otto, 11
poet figure (Lam.)
children as concern of, 50
on God as enemy warrior, 48–49, 54–55
lament for city, 42
persuasion of, 51–57
Zion interrupted by, 46, 51
Zion's interruption of, 38–39
on Zion's pain, 44–45, 91
poetry, function of, 117–18
See also medieval Hebrew poetry
"pour out," use of term, 56–57
praise, lament as transition to, 55–56, 59
prayer, lament contrasted to, 11, 55
precious things, connotation of, 40, 156–57n. 15
Provan, Iain, 16, 17
Pseudo-Jonathan, 85, 161n. 10
punishment, emphasis on, 46, 111, 164n. 52
See also guilt

Rachel
absence of, 126, 128–29
as mother, 109, 114–15
Zion compared to, 115–16, 128
rationalism, emotionalism juxtaposed to, 6–7
Rav, Joseph, 162n. 23
readers
effects of survival literature on, 21–22